CAN I SEE YOUR ID?

Discovering and Understanding Your Purpose and Identity

STAN BELYSHEV

CAN I SEE YOUR ID?

Discovering and Understanding Your

Purpose and Identity

by

Stan Belyshev

NextGen Leaders Academy

www.StanBelyshev.com

Paperback ISBN: 978-1-7352105-2-0

Kindle ISBN: 978-1-7352105-1-3

Library of Congress Control Number 2020909531

Scripture taken from the New King James Version˚. Copyright © 1982 by Thomas Nelson. Used by permission. All rights reserved.

CONTENTS

INTRODUCTION   1

PART 1

The Birth and The Origin of Your Identity and Purpose

1 CAN I SEE YOUR ID?   4

2 IT ALL BEGAN IN THE GARDEN   7

3 THE WEALTHIEST PLACE ON EARTH   10

PART 2

The Discovery, The Understanding, and The Function of Your Identity and Purpose

4   THE IDENTITY OF ADAM AND EVE   13

5   THE IDENTITY OF CAIN   18

6   THE IDENTITY OF NOAH   21

7   THE IDENTITY OF ABRAHAM AND SARAH   24

8   THE IDENTITY OF LOT   28

9   THE IDENTITY OF ESAU   33

10 THE IDENTITY OF JACOB   36

11 THE IDENTITY OF JOSEPH   40

12 THE IDENTITY OF AMRAM AND JOCHEBED   46

13 THE IDENTITY OF MOSES   49

14 THE IDENTITY OF JOSHUA AND CALEB   55

15 THE IDENTITY OF RAHAB   58

16 THE IDENTITY OF GIDEON   61

17 THE IDENTITY OF SAMSON   64

18 THE IDENTITY OF NAOMI AND RUTH   71

19 THE IDENTITY OF HANNAH   75

20 THE IDENTITY OF SAMUEL   77

21 THE IDENTITY OF KING SAUL   80

22 THE IDENTITY OF DAVID   84

23 THE IDENTITY OF SHAMMAH, ELEAZAR, JOSHEB-
    BASSHEBETH, ABISHAI, AND BENAIAH   90

24 THE IDENTITY OF ABSALOM   93

25 THE IDENTITY OF KING SOLOMON   97

26 THE IDENTITY OF ELIJAH   101

27 THE IDENTITY OF JEZEBEL   104

28 THE IDENTITY OF ELISHA   107

29 THE IDENTITY OF A YOUNG JEWISH GIRL   110

30 THE IDENTITY OF KING HEZEKIAH   114

31 THE IDENTITY OF NEHEMIAH   117

32 THE IDENTITY OF MORDECAI   122

33 THE IDENTITY OF ESTHER   125

34 THE IDENTITY OF JOB   129

35 THE IDENTITY OF DANIEL   133

36 THE IDENTITY OF SHADRACH, MESHACH,

AND ABED-NEGO 137

37 THE IDENTITY OF JONAH 141

38 THE IDENTITY OF JOHN THE BAPTIST 146

39 THE IDENTITY OF VIRGIN MARY 150

40 THE IDENTITY OF APOSTLE THOMAS 153

41 THE IDENTITY OF THE WOMAN AT THE WELL 156

42 THE IDENTITY OF THE PRODIGAL SON 159

43 THE IDENTITY OF APOSTLE PAUL 162

44 THE IDENTITY OF JUDAS ISCARIOT 169

45 THE IDENTITY OF LUCIFER 174

46 THE IDENTITY OF JESUS 180

PART 3

Protect Your Identity! Fight for Your Purpose! And Fulfill Your Kingdom Assignment on This Earth!

47 THE AGE-OLD THIEF 189

48 WE NEED TO FIGHT FOR THE NEXT GENERATION 195

49 FACTS VERSUS THE TRUTH 199

50 GOD IS THE AUTHOR OF YOUR LIFE 204

NOTES 205

INRODUCTION

Who am I? Why was I born? What is my purpose on this earth? Do I have any potential? Where am I going? Sooner or later every born individual will ask themselves these vital questions. And the discovery and the understanding of our God-given identity and purpose lays within these two fundamental principles:

Knowing your identity in Christ!
and
Knowing your identity through Christ!

When you were born, you came into this world with a personal manual called an *identity*. Now it is up to you to unlock this manual and to discover who you are and what your primary purpose on this earth is! The late Dr. Myles Munroe had a profound explanation for *purpose* as he said, "The greatest tragedy in life is not death, but a life without a purpose." Just that one statement speaks volumes to why many are simply existing and not living on this earth.

You see, the originality and the uniqueness of your physical fingerprints only confirm that you are an original masterpiece. And your identity is like a unique fingerprint that you, and only you, possess. This was divinely engraved into all of us by God our Creator. Additionally, there is a major difference between your identity *in* Christ and your identity *through* Christ. You may be wondering how this is so. The Bible is full of various metaphors where we are likened to sheep or a lion. So, your identity *in* Christ is when we are likened to sheep as we follow our Shepherd and listen to His voice, as He leads us to green pastures and to the still waters. But our identity *through* Christ is when we are likened to a lion as we boldly represent the kingdom of God on this earth as ambassadors of Christ by walking and functioning in our calling and purpose.

Discovering and understanding your God-given identity is an adventurous journey, but the process will take time, patience, humility, and your full submission and surrender to your Creator. That means that you need to trust and to come into full agreement with your Maker as to who you are, why you were created, what your purpose on this earth is, and where you are going. In other words, there are some things that absolutely every human being needs to come to accept. You must accept that God has already predestined your gender, your skin color, your geographical origin, where you were born and what specific identity and purpose He has given you. If you can come into agreement and alignment with God on these things, then you are off to a very good start.

Jesus died on the cross! Peter walked on water! The Virgin Mary gave birth to the Messiah! The young teenager, David, killed a monstrous warrior named Goliath! Joseph became second in command in Egypt! Shadrach, Meshach, and Abed-Nego went through the fiery furnace! I guess the questions I am asking you are, "What will your God-given identity and purpose do in your personal life?" and "What extraordinary adventures will you experience on this earth?"

Often there is a misconception or a lack of understanding amongst fellow Christians as it pertains to their kingdom calling or what we like to term as ministry. Your God-given assignment, identity, calling, or purpose can be characterized through your highly intellectual mind, through your physical body or physical abilities, through your mouth and the words that you speak, or through your skills, talents, or abilities. Or it could be through entrepreneurial abilities as you are able to generate much wealth. In other words, do not limit who you were created to be and what you are capable of doing to only the four walls of your local church. With that said, what is the definition of someone's kingdom identity and purpose? It is simply discovering that you are a child of God and an authorized kingdom ambassador on this earth who functions and operates in their assignment, calling, and purpose and also establishes the kingdom mandate on earth until Christ's return. Simply stated, a kingdom ambassador is an authorized individual who was washed by the blood of Jesus and received Christ as their Lord and Savior, and now has the divine authority to represent Christ and His kingdom on this earth.

Here is a thought! Water is essential for the fish so it can breathe and function at its full capacity. The wings on a bird are vital for its function so the bird can fly. The soil is crucial for every plant and tree to reside in so they can grow and live. And oxygen is vital for every human being, so we can breathe and survive. But if you take the fish out of water, it will die. If you cut off the bird's wings, it will no longer fly. If you uproot a plant or a tree from the ground, it will eventually wither and die. And if oxygen is absent in the atmosphere, then every human being and many other things will also die. This principle is also true when it comes to your kingdom identity and purpose on this earth. Those who do not know or have not discovered their God-given identity and purpose are simply existing, not living.

As you venture through the pages of this book, in Part 1, you will be introduced to the birth and the origin of your God-given identity and purpose. In Part 2, you will encounter numerous biblical characters, and as you uncover their kingdom identity and purpose, you will, in the process, begin to understand and to grasp much clarity for your own God-given identity, and purpose. And finally, in Part 3, you will be challenged to protect your identity, to fight for your purpose, and to fulfill your kingdom assignment on this earth.

PART 1
The Birth and The Origin of Your Identity and Purpose

1
CAN I SEE YOUR ID?

C an I see your ID? Yes! No! Maybe! Not Sure! What were you asking again? ID is an abbreviation for the word *identification* which is defined as the following: something that identifies a person; or the state of being identified, or described.[1] In one of my recent travels through Europe, I travelled through five different countries, and whether by plane, through the airport, or while crossing the border in a vehicle, I was oftentimes asked for my passport, which was to confirm who I was and where I was from, or my personal identity.

The identification concept is very similar when it comes to our state driver's license, which is also requested when we need to show proof of our age, name, or while making financial transactions or signing off on important documents. In other words, your driver's license or your passport is a tool that establishes your identity, not because you don't know who you are, but to satisfy those who are requesting such legal identification.

In this case, the question, "Can I See Your ID?", does not refer to your governmental identification but to your kingdom identification. So, do you know your kingdom identity? Are you a kingdom citizen? What kingdom rights do you have on this earth? What is your kingdom purpose? For what reason were you born? Are you a child of God? And if you were to die right now, would you be in the presence of your heavenly Father, or would you be condemned for eternity to the lake of fire? All the above questions need to be seriously considered as they are related to your identity *in* Christ and your identity *through* Christ.

Your Identity *in* Christ and Your Identity *through* Christ

Your God-given identity is hidden in the *image* and in the *likeness* of your heavenly Father.[2] And there is a big difference between your identity *in* Christ and your identity *through* Christ! Allow me to elaborate:

4

My Identity in Christ: Is knowing that you are a son or a daughter of God and that the blood of Jesus has washed away all of your sins, and because of the death and the resurrection of Christ, you have been reconciled with your heavenly Father. And when you die, you will spend eternity with Him in His presence. This first phase solely pertains to you in reference to your salvation, redemption, and eternity.

My Identity through Christ: Is discovering and understanding your kingdom assignment, calling, and purpose on this earth. This consists of knowing your gifts, potential, skills, and or discovering your inner passion for what most captivates your heart, your mind, and your attention. This second phase solely pertains to what you need to do while you are living on this earth.

Here is something for you to ponder. If Tiger Woods traded places with Lebron James for one season, how would Tiger Woods play basketball and how successful would Lebron James be at golf? Or how about Tom Brady trading places with Derek Jeter? How successful would they be? As much as each athlete may excel in their specific sport, playing another sport does not mean they will be successful. In like manner, we as God's children excel and function the best in our God-given identity and purpose.

Too many Christians Believers get caught up in the mindset or theology that the more they pray, fast, or read the Bible, the greater the anointing they will have, resulting in more influence and more success in ministry and in life. There is some truth to that! But why is it that so many Believers become so discouraged in their walk in the Lord as it specifically relates to their purpose and calling? Are they not praying or fasting enough?

Some of my biggest frustrations were not because I did not pray enough, read enough, or fast enough, it was because I did not fully know or understand my God-given identity and purpose. If Lebron James decided to practice hard every day in baseball he would still never be as good at it as somebody like Derek Jeter. We saw this illustrated with Michael Jordan who decided to retire from basketball and play baseball instead. He was not very successful.

To stress my point further, God did not call or anoint us, nor has He equipped us to do absolutely everything and anything! And that is why it is up to us, with the help of the Holy Spirit and God's Word, and through the prayer and guidance of other individuals, to discover our gifts, abilities, and talents that make up our calling. And most importantly, to discover our God-given identity and purpose for our life on this earth.

Myths about Your Identity and Purpose

Often, we allow individuals to construct in our hearts and in the subconscious part of our minds, some myths regarding our identity and purpose. Let us take a look at some of these myths:

- You have to become a certain age in order to understand or to discover your identity and purpose.
- You have to be fully mature in order to start operating in your purpose and calling.
- You need to be involved or have some kind of ministry in your local church.
- You need someone in spiritual authority like a pastor to pray over you in order for you to know your God-given identity and purpose.
- You will not need anyone else in your life to help you to fulfill your purpose and assignment.
- Your calling or purpose is limited or restricted to a certain geographical location.
- You need to receive a prophetic word over your life or have a specific dream or vision.
- You can miss out on knowing your identity and purpose.

Always remember that our heavenly Father does not experiment with our lives, especially as it pertains to our identity and purpose. You see, much confusion has and continues to arise amongst Christians as it relates to someone's identity and kingdom assignment and purpose. Why? Usually, it is because of extreme theology or narrow-minded understanding. For example, some stress more praying, fasting, and servanthood in the local church to discover your purpose, but many who do those things are still confused about their life. Or some will say that you need to experiment, or venture out, or take continuous risks and that will help you to know your purpose. Either one has its own extremes, limitations, and risks. Their needs to be a healthy balance.

2
IT ALL BEGAN IN THE GARDEN

L ucifer's first attack on mankind was not on wealth or health or possessions. His first attack was aimed at Adam and Eve's identity. The serpent said, "Has God indeed said, 'You shall not eat of every tree of the garden?'"[1] The body of Christ and countless Christians have been blindsided through ignorance by thinking that the enemy of our soul is mainly targeting our health, our finances, our children and our evangelistic outreaches. All the devil needs to do is strip off our God-given identity and he has already accomplished more than we realize.

Here are a few thought-provoking insights that we all need to seriously consider from this very short but a generationally deadly conversation that the serpent had with Eve:

- Never try to have a dialog with the devil! When you do, you will be deceived.
- The moment you incline your ears to the voice of the devil will be the moment when you bite into his bait, and it is just a matter of time until he lures you like a fish with a hook in its mouth.
- The serpent did not fully lie to Eve! He just did not tell her about the consequences of disobeying God since he was already experienced in that area.

Adam and Eve Were Stripped Naked from Their God-Given Identity

We can easily get carried away from the understanding that Adam and Eve were already naked, and the innocent Sunday school teachers don't always touch on the deeper meaning of their nakedness. The fact that Adam and Eve never knew that they were naked until they ate of the forbidden fruit should already provide for us a big clue. Let's observe a powerful dialog that God had with them when they committed their first sin: "I heard Your voice in the garden, and I was afraid because I was naked; and I hid myself."[2] In response, God said, "Who told you that you were naked?"[3]

7

Sin and disobedience to God's Word will automatically strip you naked and make you vulnerable before our enemy. For example, whenever any of my three children disobey and get themselves into trouble, then, as any normal parent would do, I will discipline them. Not because we hate our child but because we love them and want to teach them a valuable lesson. In like manner, our heavenly Father also disciplines us out of love, but that also means that He is faithful to His own Word and whenever we live in rebellion or opposition to His Word, then it will be the Word that will judge us. That is why Adam and Eve became shamefully naked, because they disobeyed God's Word.

Hostility Between the Seeds

Back in 2006 I bought a book which had the very intriguing title of *Enmity Between the Seeds*, written by Bill Cloud. It was a little book, but it was packed with a spiritual punch! The preface of the whole book outlines that the seed of the serpent, will always be at war with the seed of God. In other words, the children of Satan will continually resist the children of God.

Satan, the serpent, never rests and is continually sowing his seeds of deception, corruption, envy, hatred, fear, and accusations against the children of God. And if we allow any of his demonic seeds to be sown into our hearts, into our minds, or into our spirit man, then it will only be a matter of time until they will sprout forth and usher in their specified purpose, and that purpose is destruction.

The serpent was successful as he sowed his deceptive seed into the heart of Eve, and his age-old tactics still pollute the hearts of millions. For us, as God's children, we should never be ignorant that for as long as we live on this earth, we will always have hostility between the seeds. But knowing our God-given identity and purpose will allow us to have great victory over our enemy and bring down every thought or stronghold that is brought against us.

Has God Indeed Said?

"Now the serpent was more cunning than any beast of the field which the Lord God had made. And he said to the woman, 'Has God indeed said, "You shall not eat of every tree of the garden"'?"[4] These four words have destroyed millions upon millions of lives:

- *Has God indeed said* that you are beautiful?
- *Has God indeed said* that you will be successful?

- *Has God indeed said* that you are blessed?
- *Has God indeed said* that you have a purpose?
- *Has God indeed said* that you have a hope and a future?
- *Has God indeed said* that you are forgiven?
- *Has God indeed said* that you are His child?
- *Has God indeed said* you will be in eternity with Him?
- *Has God indeed said* that He will take away all of your fears and worries?

Yes, God already said that you are beautiful! Yes, you are successful! Yes, you are blessed! Yes, you do have a purpose! And yes, you will spend all of eternity with Him! These are not meant to be attractive, motivational statements that are written throughout the Word of God but are the truths that God is speaking into the hearts of mankind. Yes, God indeed said what He said, and yes, He will do and fulfill all of what He has already said. God is not a man that He should lie, and He cannot contradict His own Word.

The identity crisis of humanity originated in the Garden of Eden, but because of the sacrifice and the fulfilled kingdom assignment of Jesus Christ, every living human being no longer needs to live in this spiritual identity crisis. And if you feel naked and afraid, then come to your Creator with humility and repentance so He can clothe you with His divine identity and also reveal to you your kingdom purpose.

3
THE WEALTHIEST PLACE ON EARTH

A llow me to start off with a very profound question. What is the wealthiest place on earth? Is it the diamond fields of Africa? Is it the oil fields of Saudi Arabia? Is it Dubai with all of its glamour and glory? Or how about the Swiss Bank? From the natural perspective, all of the above are credible sources, but in reality, the wealthiest place on earth is the cemetery. This profound insight and powerful revelation was oftentimes shared by the late Dr. Myles Munroe.

Diamonds, gold, or any other precious metals will never be valuable for as long as they stay buried or hidden beneath the earth. Unpublished books, or unproduced movies, or undiscovered scientific breakthroughs likewise will never be valuable or in demand for as long as they remain dormant within that particular individual. And this is why the cemetery happens to be the wealthiest place on earth. Why? Because too much of untapped and unreleased God-given potential and purpose is buried there.

Spiritual Abortion

Recently, abortion has been a hot topic for the news media and has also been at the center of various political debates. But in this section, I want to outline the vital importance on how, with no significant effort, millions upon millions have aborted and continue to abort their kingdom identity and purpose.

The discovery of your God-given identity is very similar to a woman's pregnancy cycle. In the earlier phase of pregnancy, most women do not know that they're pregnant until something begins to happen in their body. They may feel nauseous, a loss of appetite, mood swings, or other uncomfortable symptoms. This is also true when you begin to discover your God-given identity and purpose, something begins to happen in your heart, in your spirit, in your mind, and in your thinking. You may also begin to daydream or go into trances about something specific.

But just like any normal and healthy pregnancy requires a full nine-month cycle, it also requires a full cycle to discover your purpose. But a pregnancy where the child is born early is considered a premature birth and many times a premature birth comes with health risks and other side effects. In similar manner, when you have not fully understood your God-given identity and purpose and you try to walk it out or operate in it prematurely, it could eventually backfire on you and cause more devastation and discouragement rather than becoming a great blessing.

Even more tragically, too many Believers have aborted their God-given identity and purpose because they did not originally discover and understand the hidden potential and treasure that was lying within their heart and spirit man. And their procrastination, wrong life choices, wasting valuable time, and even disobeying God, resulted in the abortion of their spiritual identity.

Are You the Potter or the Clay?

The Word of God has numerous references that our heavenly Father is the potter and we are the clay. But with that said, are you fulfilling the role of the potter or the clay? This is not a rhetorical question, since we often think that we are the potter (God) and blindly forget that we are simple clay in the hands of the almighty God. The reason I chose to title this section as I did is because we have the tendency to play the role of God, and when this occurs we are shocked when we end up with a misshapen life.

The question, "Are you the potter or the clay?" is meant to be a reality check. Because, as long as we try to fulfill the role of the Potter, we will continually resist the hand of God in and over our lives as He desires to shape and to form us into His image and into His likeness.

As I wrap up "Part I" of this book, you will next find yourself on an extraordinary journey through the lives of fifty-four biblical characters who will guide you on discovering, understanding, and releasing your God-given identity and purpose on this earth. Some of these biblical characters portray a negative identity and purpose, which also plays a crucial role in guiding you in the right direction. Do pay close attention to how unique and how special each and every biblical character is and how their particular identity reflects into your personal life and into your God-given identity and purpose.

PART 2
The Discovery, the Understanding, and The Function of Your Identity and Purpose

4

THE IDENTITY OF ADAM AND EVE

Has God Indeed Said?

W hen we try to evaluate the life of Adam and Eve in detail, the first created human beings, we come across a little dilemma! The dilemma is that we are limited to about three short chapters in the book of Genesis and a few other references in the New Testament. I guess our honest and fair argument before God could be, "Why were we limited to such a small outline to the life of these incredible human beings?"

The "Identity of Adam and Eve" is an essential revelation that every child of God needs to grasp—more than any other biblical personae, with the exception of Jesus. The original human DNA and the kingdom identity was engraved in Adam and it was naturally passed on from generation to generation, until this day.

As you venture through this chapter, you will learn of two remarkable individuals who were the original blueprint for all of humanity, and here you will discover valuable lessons from the life and purpose of Adam and Eve. In this chapter, you will learn why your identity is unique and full of creativity and potential. You will also learn how you will be challenged by the enemy of your soul to believe whether God said what He said about you or not. And finally, we should not get carried away by trying to play the blame game but to take full responsibility over our life, over our choices, and over our purpose.

Creativity and innovation are derived from your identity and it becomes manifested through your purpose.

Your Identity Has A Unique Creativity and Potential

I could only imagine how much fun our heavenly Father had with Adam. First, the Bible does not specify when God created Eve, so Adam could've been alone for a while. Second, God placed Adam in the garden and gave him his first responsibility, to *tend* and to *keep* the garden. But then, something interesting occurred where God wanted Adam to begin to release his untapped potential which was already embedded into his inner identity.

God brought every beast of the field and every bird of the air before Adam and challenged Adam to name all of them. This moment is one of the most powerful demonstrations of the Father's divine desire to spend quality time with His children, just like any earthly parent would with their child. This moment is recorded with these words, "Out of the ground the Lord God formed every beast of the field and every bird of the air, and brought *them* to Adam to see what he would call them."[1] This occasion is truly special as God was very curious to see what His creation would do, just like any parent would be curious to see their child trying to do something for the first time.

As Adam began to name all of the animals, the Scripture records this profound statement, "And whatever Adam called each living creature, that *was* its name."[2] Did you grasp that? In other words, God never interfered with Adam's decision and God did not go back and rename some of those creatures. Also, allow this additional wild thought to sink in: whatever name that Adam gave to those creatures, we are still calling those same creatures by their original name they received from Adam. So today, a lion, a bear, an ant, or a dove was originally named by Adam, not by scientists or biologists or explorers. Now that is awesome!

The lesson here is that each and every living human being has embedded into their identity this same unique creativity that we all need to discover and release. Some of the challenges to this is that when we do discover our unique identity, we become intimidated, doubtful, and even begin to question it. Why? Because it may look weird, or you may not know anyone within your inner circle who has this similar desire or gift, or you may think that others will laugh at you or think that you are weird.

I have personally experienced all of the above and still continue to come across folks who give me that awkward look. One of those areas is in my book writing. Oftentimes, people who know me would ask what I am doing for ministry, and one of my responses is, "I write books!" And this is when these folks would give me "that look." Why? Because that is usually not their interpretation or understanding of what ministry is. This usually is a great opportunity to explain to that particular person why God has uniquely granted us with various gifts. I explain that we each have creativity that we need to discover and then begin to release for His kingdom purpose.

This phenomenal encounter that occurred between God and Adam is majestic, and this similar encounter needs to occur with every born-again Believer where they discover what potential, gifting, talent, or abilities are lying dormant within them. When we begin to unlock these creative abilities, the anointing on our life is what will give this inner creativity tangible credibility and worth before others.

Your identity will continually be challenged and attacked by the enemy of your soul.

Has God Indeed Said?

The serpent in the garden initiated and activated a deceptive challenge, which is still so powerfully effective to this day, when he said to Eve, "Has God indeed said?"[3] This demonic statement continues to numb and confuse the hearts and the minds of every born-again believer. It is also this same phrase that has tragically stripped away the God-given identity from numerous individuals, just like it exposed the nakedness of Adam and Eve.

In my early years as a fresh born-again believer, I was also on the path of searching for my God-given identity and purpose. And during this journey, I have heard a similar phrase more than once, "Did God really say such and such?" This usually occurred while I was ready to boldly step forward or to function in my purpose or whenever I would go through a transitional season of my life. Either way, this demonic whisper would usually bring confusion, fear, doubt, and slowly rob my faith.

Has God indeed said? Are you sure that you heard from the Lord? How certain are you that it was the Holy Spirit that prompted your heart? Or maybe it was just your emotional intuition. Was that a prophetic word from God or just a word from a person's good spiritual intentions? All of these questions continually bombard every born-again believer. This is nothing that we need to be afraid of or try to run away from, since it is in these moments of your spiritual life that the Holy Spirit is actually training us to discern who is speaking to you, and in the process, you also begin to grow stronger in the Lord.

15

You would think that Adam and Eve were very well equipped to resist and to ignore the deceptive tactics and the lies of the serpent. I honestly do believe that they were, but their weakness or downfall is a powerful lesson for all Believers that the serpent is cunning and very tactful. Adam and Eve also exemplify the truth that we should never have a dialog with the enemy of our soul, and this usually occurs whenever we begin to entertain the age-old challenge, "Did God really say?"

Knowing your purpose will keep you accountable and steadfast before others.

Don't Play the Blame Game

When Adam and Eve sinned, they both played the *Blame Game* before the Lord. Adam blamed Eve, and Eve blamed the serpent. What occurred at this moment does portray a classic example of what many of us do today. When life comes crashing down, we blame our spouse. When we lose our job, or face a dire financial deficit, we bombard God with endless *why* questions: "Why me God?" Or, "Why are You not answering my prayers?" It is amazing how quickly and easily we try to point the blame on someone or something else, but never take full responsibility over our unpleasant circumstance.

I wonder with much curiosity that if only Adam and Eve had, at that moment, taken full responsibility over their actions and asked God for forgiveness, if the outcome would have been totally different. Would they still remain in the garden? Would God forgive them, and apply another form of discipline? I believe that something different would have come out of this, since whenever we ask God for forgiveness because of our disobedience or stupidity, God does forgive us. And sure, in the process we may get a gentle slap on our spiritual butt-cheeks.

Playing the *Blame Game* will only dig a deeper hole for you yourself to fall into. Also, whenever you try to play this game, always remember that you will always end up losing. Always! Numerous born-again Believers have tragically jeopardized their purpose and calling on this earth, simply because they chose to point their *blame* finger at someone else and not take full responsibility.

From just this short chapter we can definitely learn very powerful life lessons from Adam and Eve, who were both students in the making and at the same time teachers, who could teach us much about our identity and our purpose. The identity of Adam and Eve still speaks loud and clear into the hearts of every child of God, since what occurred in their life, as we read in just three short chapters, is very sound and profound.

The day you discover your God-given identity will be the day when you give birth to your purpose.

Takeaway Lessons from the Life of Adam and Eve

- Your identity will let you know how original and how unique you are.
- Your identity and purpose will have a strategic attack from the enemy of your soul, the devil.
- Your identity will surprisingly be challenged by the Word of God, which will be taken out of its context by the enemy of your soul.

5

THE IDENTITY OF CAIN
Your Heart Does Matter

C ain was privileged to have been the first human being that was born through the natural process of conception, where Adam's seed impregnated Eve. This was the first and one of the most powerful God-given privileges that our heavenly Father has bestowed upon the human race where we have the ability and the power to bring forth another living human being into the existence of our world. In other words, God distributed a portion of His creative power into the man, Adam, in the form of a seed, and a portion of His creative power into the woman, Eve, in the form of a womb.

I remember years ago when the Holy Spirit gave me a revelation about the privilege we have of obtaining certain Godly creative power, as it relates to bringing another living human being into this world. This revelation transformed my thinking and has also allowed for me to see God's promises for His children in a whole different spectrum.

In this chapter, you will learn from the life of the first naturally conceived and birthed individual who also did the unthinkable. You will also grasp the understanding that our heavenly Father is more focused on your heart, rather than your purpose or calling.

Your purpose will challenge you to have a clean heart.

Cain Committed the Unthinkable

The story of Cain is tragic as he was recorded as the first human being to have killed another human being, who happened to be his blood-born brother, Abel. No, God did not turn His back on Cain and still had a purpose for him, but I do want to point out another important life lesson for us to seriously ponder, which I call the *spirit of Cain*:

- Born-again Believers can and have committed unthinkable atrocities, which brought harm to other individuals and some have even ended up in prison.
- Just because you are saved, or you regularly attend church, or you can quote numerous Bible passages does not make you exempt from committing horrible, devastating, or unthinkable things.
- Way too many husbands who consider themselves as born-again Believers have physically abused their wives. And an unaccountable number of spouses have committed sexual affairs with others.
- Relationships that should be loving are hurt and broken because of scenarios such as the following: siblings hating or despising each other, children dishonoring and even suing their parents, and family members refusing to forgive and not talking to one another for decades.
- We are witnessing more and more church leaders who are splitting the church in half and opening their own churches. Or church leaders fighting with each other over pathetic things, which causes much dishonor towards the senior pastor.

This *spirit of Cain* is oftentimes because sin lays within the heart of the individual. God said to Cain, "Sin lies at the door,"[1] and through this rebuke, God was signifying to Cain that his heart is out of spiritual alignment. Whenever sin of fleshly desires lays at the door of your heart, then it will affect you in your personal life, in your spiritual walk, and will also become manifested in the ministry.

Yes, Cain was able to do the unthinkable, just like any of us are able to do horrific things, but this should never become a tangible or a justifiable reason for anyone to think that God would turn His back on you. For as long as you humbly come before God with repentance, He will be able to fully restore you from any foolish act or stupid choices that you have made in your life.

Knowing your identity and purpose will give you the heart of servanthood.

God Is More Focused on Your Heart Rather Than on Your Calling or Purpose

One of Cain's primary issues was that he was more focused on his daily works, rather than on keeping his heart clean and sinless. Apostle Paul once gave the Galatians a reminder by saying, "Knowing that a man is not justified by the works of the law but by faith in Jesus Christ, even we have believed in Christ Jesus, that we might be justified by faith in Christ and not by the works of the law; for by the works of the law no flesh shall be justified."[2]

As tragic as Cain's life turned out, we still are witnessing similar patterns taking place in the body of Christ by Believers who are more focused on their works, rather than keeping their hearts pure and clean. Usually, the enemy of our souls' preys upon many by influencing them to focus more on what they can do for the Lord, rather than keeping their heart spiritually healthy. Martha is another great example of an individual who was sincerely occupied by getting some food ready for Jesus, while Mary sat at His feet. It is not a sin to do good things for others and for God's kingdom, but that should never have more priority over keeping your heart and your spiritual walk with the Lord healthy. And the heart of God powerfully demonstrates this principle.

The life story of Cain may be tragic, but not without hope. Just like Cain, we will make foolish, stupid, or even consequential mistakes, but this is not the end of the world. We need to learn to come back to our Creator and allow Him to bring our life back into its proper position.

When your identity and purpose is not discovered, then your value for others becomes irrelevant.

Takeaway Lessons from the Life of Cain

- Knowing your identity and purpose will help you to keep your heart right and will also help you to value others in a similar way as God does.
- Your identity and purpose are not meant to be occupied by your works, or even by your kingdom assignment. But to always make sure that your heart stands in the right spiritual alignment.
- Those who experience an identity crisis become very vulnerable to making devastating life choices.

6
THE IDENTITY OF NOAH
Why Is It Taking So Long?

T he life and story of Noah still has to be one of the most favorite parts of the Bible taught to children around the whole world. And not only that, even Ken Ham who was so captivated by God's phenomenal creativity as it relates to Noah building that ark, opened a theme park in 2016 called The Ark Encounter, which has a replica of a massive-sized ark that spans 510 feet long, 85 feet wide, and 51 feet high. The story of the ark which millions upon millions of people have read about, we now have the opportunity to see in person.

I and my best friend have partnered together in a business venture building and selling custom homes and one of the most exiting phases of the whole construction has to be the framing. Once the framing goes up, you then begin to see the characteristics of the house. We are also able to complete the whole framing process in about ten days. Now this was not the case for Noah who did not have the manpower, the modern-day tools, or the experience that we do today. But he did have plenty of time as it took him more than one hundred years to build the ark. In this chapter, you will learn about patience, the timing of the Lord, and to never let down your guard.

Just like you cannot rush the metamorphosis process of the caterpillar, likewise you cannot rush emergence of your purpose. God's timing is always perfect.

Why Is It Taking So Long?

Noah should receive the credit for inventing the word *patience*. It took Noah more than one hundred years to build the ark. Building this ark was the assignment and purpose that he needed to fulfill. Yes, Noah did live for 950 years, so he definitely had all the time in the world, but he was also limited to the same twenty-four-hour days as we are and to only one life on earth.

Waiting with patience is not a virtue that anyone naturally possesses! But this is something that is inevitable for us all. A pregnant woman needs to patiently wait for her full nine-month pregnancy to come to fruition before she gives birth, or else a pre-mature baby will come with many potential complications or health issues. A restaurant customer needs to patiently wait for their meal order or else the waiter or the waitress will serve them a raw or an uncooked meal. And we as God's children need to patiently wait for God's will, purpose, and timing to come to its proper alignment without us trying to do things by ourselves, which could have dire consequences. In other words, we do not want to give birth to an Ishmael, like Abraham did.

Noah can definitely teach us that waiting upon the Lord is vital and that what He has entrusted us with will eventually came to pass. God is more interested in our success and in the fulfilment of our assignment than we ever will be. And sooner or later, everyone will ask the same age-old question: Why is this taking so long?

The discovery or the understanding of your God-given identity could take some time.

Long Preparation for A Short Assignment

It took Noah more than one hundred years of preparation for an assignment that lasted for 230 days, until the rains stopped, and the water fully receded. This could be very frustrating for many of us when we prepare for years for something that lasts for one season or even one day. You plan for months for a conference or a big church event that only lasts for one day. You plan up to a year for your special wedding day, that only lasts for less than one day. And you go to college for up to four years, or longer, so you can obtain the needed education or diploma in order to pass through a one-hour job interview, so you can land yourself a dream career.

You see, God is not in the business of microwaving our kingdom assignment, and He definitely does not want us to have a microwave attitude since He is a God of order and a God of excellence. The kingdom of God is a kingdom of high standards, quality, and excellence. And we should never deceive ourselves by foolishly thinking that we can just simply lay all of the responsibilities upon the Holy Spirit or upon the anointing. This type of immature thinking has made the body of Christ look foolish, irrelevant, and uninfluential. Yes, your preparation could take some time for only a short

22

assignment, but trust in the Lord and do not lean unto your fleshly understanding. And while waiting, do not let your guard down.

Purpose was given to us before we were born, but it could take a lifetime for us to fulfill it.

Never Let Down Your Guard

As the only living human beings on the face of the earth and with so much land and so much abundance of whatever the heart would desire, Noah began to farm the land and eventually got drunk with wine. In his drunkenness he lay naked in his tent, which resulted in his shameful and embarrassing exposure before his sons. Sadly enough, we are continually bombarded with stories of pastors or preachers or other well-known ministers who fell into sin or into shameful conduct. Whenever we lay down our guard, the enemy of our soul will strip us naked and expose us before others, especially before our family members, our friends and other fellow Believers.

Our calling and potential will usher into our lives many blessings, much material gain, or influence before others, but we should always stay humble and be at guard to make sure that we do not become drunk from the fruit of our labor, just like Noah did. And finally, don't grow tired or weary as you patiently wait upon the Lord and for His perfect timing as He divinely orchestrates everything and everyone into their proper configuration to make sure that you will be able to fulfill your kingdom assignment on this earth.

Your identity is like a personal bodyguard that is meant to keep you safe and to make sure that you securely make it to your final destination.

Takeaway Lessons from the Life of Noah

- Your purpose could take a while until it is fulfilled.
- Your kingdom assignment could be for a specific season, for a specific geographical area, or for a specific time.
- Your calling will require much patience and fully trusting in the Lord's timing.

7
THE IDENTITY OF ABRAHAM AND SARAH
All Things Are Possible

The life of Abraham and Sarah is very unique and I could also add that they both qualify as the coolest elderly couple in the Bible. In accordance to our modern-day medical technology and breakthroughs, it is still very impossible for a ninety-year-old woman to get pregnant, but because God had a specific purpose, Sarah defied all the laws of nature and physics.

Before Abraham and Sarah understood their God-given identity and purpose, they were called Abram and Sarai. But when Abram was ninety-nine years old, the Lord appeared to him and said that He would multiply him and his descendants like the sand on the shore and the stars in the heavens. God also changed their names to Abraham and Sarah.

Abraham: means father of many nations
Sarah: means princess

At first, Abraham argued with God and used his old age and the fact that he was also childless as an excuse on how he could not be a father of many nations. But God had other plans for him and Sarah, so when he broke the news to his wife, Sarah laughed herself silly. And in this chapter, you will take a walk through the lives of Abraham and Sarah and in the process discover that God is not intimidated or restricted by time, age, or world circumstances. Why? Because with God, all things are possible.

Identity and purpose do not go on retirement.

It Is Never Too Late to Fulfill Your God-Given Purpose and Assignment

How does Abraham and Sarah's identity resemble our own lives? Some of you might have already placed a tombstone over your life, just because of your older age or because you think that it is too late for you to move forward with the original promises, dreams, or visions that God has birthed in your heart and spirit man.

As a child of God, always remember that it is never too late to fulfill your God-given purpose and assignment on this earth. But, if you are eagerly looking forward to your retirement, then you have not discovered your purpose, since it is your purpose that continually gives you the inner drive to keep on moving forward. Additionally, ponder on this powerful thought: if you don't take charge of your personal time, then someone else will.

Identity will become like a compass in your life as it guides you into the right direction.

Do Not Give Birth to a Man-Made Identity

Abraham thought that God made a mistake by promising him a son, so after he had consulted with his wife Sarah, they gave birth to Ishmael, as Abraham impregnated the servant Hagar. As much as this deed of Abraham sounded so weird and strange, we can take away a powerful life lesson here. The lesson is, do not give birth to a man-made identity. Somehow Abraham and Sarah thought that they could help God by making sure that His promise to them would come to pass, but by doing so, they gave birth to a man-made identity by the name of Ishmael.

We all would be making a dire mistake by judging Abraham and Sarah with the foolish choice that they made, but the truth is that many of us have given birth to our own types of Ishmaelites in our own lives. This usually occurs whenever we begin to lose trust in our heavenly Father, or when we begin to stray away from His divine will for our life. Remember, for as long as you place your faith and trust in the Lord's promises for you, you then will avoid giving birth to a man-made identity by the name of Ishmael.

It will be very difficult for you to successfully add value to others; to lead others; and to influence others, until you have discovered your inner identity and purpose.

Your Purpose and Kingdom Assignment Has a Generational Impact

God told Abraham that He would multiply his descendants like the stars in the heavens and like the sand on the seashore. God's original promise to Abraham is so evident in our time and in our generation, as we now have Believers in Christ all over the whole world.

You see, your purpose and kingdom assignment have a generational impact. What God originally promised to Abraham, thousands of years later, His promise is more and more evident. Oftentimes we become ignorant to the fact that our God-given purpose has a generational impact. And many times, you may not witness the fruits of your kingdom assignment during your lifetime, but the seeds that you will sow in your generational season will definitely give fruit in the next generation.

Your kingdom purpose is not limited by your age, or by a geographical area, or by your societal status.

Your Kingdom Assignment Will Be Ruthlessly Tested

Abraham's kingdom assignment was tested in an unspeakable way when God told him to offer up his promised son. "Now it came to pass after these things that God tested Abraham, and said to him, 'Abraham!' And he said, 'Here I am.' Then He said, 'Take now your son, your only *son* Isaac, whom you love, and go to the land of Moriah, and offer him there as a burnt offering on one of the mountains of which I shall tell you.'"[1] Just like Abraham was ruthlessly tested, in like manner, you will also be tested. Why? Well, first of all, the whole Bible is full of tests, trials, and tribulation. And also, the agonizing crucifixion of Jesus once again underlines a powerful truth that pain and suffering is part of your Christian walk with the Lord.

Please consider that the purity and the quality of gold and silver only becomes visible after they are placed under extreme fiery temperatures. This then results in the manufacturing of precious jewelry. Car manufacturers test the safety of their new models by driving them into solid block walls or having another dummy car slam into its side. This results in an analysis of the safety of the car for passengers and could result in saving their lives. And absolutely every product sold by companies is tested before it leaves the manufacturer's production department. Some of these tests are more strenuous than others. You may wonder why there is so much testing. If any product is defected, malfunctioning, or causes harm, the client will be dissatisfied. If this continues, the demand for that particular product could severely drop, possibly resulting in the manufacturers going out of business because of too many recalls, lawsuits, and loss of profits.

For example, the teenager David refused to use King Saul's armor, because David had not tested them.[2] Job was tested in an unthinkable way when in one day, he lost all of his children, his health, and all of his livelihood.[3] Daniel was tested in the lion's den and his three friends were tested in the fiery furnace. And throughout the whole Bible we see reference after reference of those whom the Lord tested.

The sole purpose your kingdom assignment needs to be tested is to make sure that you become more mature, faithful, committed, and that you obtain needed experience. And this is not a one-time test, but a continual testing that will occur throughout your whole life, until your dying breath. Because our heavenly Father loves us and has entrusted us with His kingdom assignment is why we have gone, we are going, and will continue to go through various trials, testing, and tribulations. And the kingdom assignment of Abraham and Sarah underlines this truthful principle.

You can always retire from a job, but you can never retire from your purpose.

Takeaway Lessons from the Life of Abraham and Sarah

- Your identity will eventually give you the true meaning of who you are and what you were called to do.
- Your identity and purpose will never be hindered by your age or other life circumstances.
- Your purpose is so significant that no excuse will ever exempt you from not fulfilling it.

8
THE IDENTITY OF LOT
Life Choices Matter

The life of Lot is not something that we would be jealous of or something that we can admire, but it is definitely a life we need to learn from. Lot's life and his particular tragic storyline should not be ignored since his life reflects much on our daily decision making and on the importance of the family unit.

The identity of Lot reflects three particular attributes or life lessons that we all can take away. First is our everyday choices. Second is our attraction towards the appetites of Sodom and Gomorrah. And finally, the third is the importance and the role of a family. Our everyday choices will determine our tomorrow. Our desire or the appetites for the world will usher in dire consequences. And whenever you sacrifice your family over your personal desires, then you have made yourself into a selfish, self-centered, and egotistic individual.

In this profound chapter, I will address the importance of discovering your kingdom assignment and purpose through your heart and not by what you see. Also, I will cover why it is so vital for you to turn away from the attractions of Sodom and Gomorrah. And finally, why the enemy of our soul is in full force by trying to destroy the family unit.

Knowing your kingdom identity will give you a clear understanding of what particular sphere you need to occupy and to influence.

Your Purpose and Kingdom Assignment Will Be Discovered through Your Heart and Not through Your Eyes

Lot's name is very unique and can be characterized in a humorous way when we remember that Abraham gave Lot a choice to either go to the right or to the left by choosing which land he would prefer to possess. And as the story goes,

Lot, of course, chose the best lot of land that was well watered and more pleasant to the eye.[1]

Your life could either become a stagnant parking lot or a valuable real estate lot. Those who have not discovered their God-given identity and purpose are stuck in a parking lot doing circles, while those who have discovered their God-given identity and purpose are actually building something of value and worth on their real estate lot. Yes, your identity and purpose possess much value and worth, but the question remains whether you will discover that value and worth or not.

I am reminded of the powerful true-life story written by Russell Conwell called *Acres of Diamonds,* where one farmer decided to find riches elsewhere and sold his farm land, only to learn that the person who bought it discovered numerous black stones which turned out to be rare diamonds. This story speaks loud and clear in reference to many that possess an inner diamond of great value and worth, and the way for you to discover it is through your heart and not by what you see.

The discovery of your identity will turn your parking lot life into a valuable real estate lot.

You Must Turn Away from the Attraction of Sodom and Gomorrah

The Bible is full of intriguing stories and supernatural occurrences. One of these has to be when Lot's wife turned into a pillar of salt as she disobeyed the commandment of the angels and turned around to look at the burning cities of Sodom and Gomorrah. This illustration has to be one of the clearest examples to us of why it is important for us to turn away from the worldly lifestyle and from all secular appetites and attractions that seem popular and relevant.

As much as the story of Lot's wife is tragic, this similar phenomenon is sweeping through our nation and throughout the whole world. The lustful appetites that are being served through modern-day Sodom and Gomorrah are off the charts. And the identity of Lot also needs to teach us the truth that God is a righteous God, and that He will not tolerate immorality and wickedness. Those who think all is well as they indulge themselves in perversion, sexual promiscuity, and immoral living or try to hide their sinful lifestyle as they regularly attend church or pridefully call themselves a Christian, would be making a tragic mistake. If you genuinely desire to walk in the fullness of your calling and purpose, then you must turn away from the attractions of Sodom and Gomorrah.

You have to fight for your purpose and for those things that you were chosen to fulfill on this earth.

The Destruction of the Family Unit

The life story of Lot and his family also portrays another tragedy that we are observing in our current culture and that is the destruction of the family unit. Like never before, we are witnessing a fierce and a demonic attack on God's originally designed family unit, which is one man and one woman united in holy matrimony without having children out of wedlock. The demonic system today, which is functioning like Sodom and Gomorrah, is undeniable, but here I want to place more emphasis on Lot and on his family situation.

Lot was very aware of the culture of Sodom and Gomorrah, but he still chose to live there. Lot also understood the dangers of the unhealthy environment of those two cities, but he still chose to raise his children there. And when the two angels came to warn Lot, this is how he replied to them, "Here now, my lords, please turn in to your servant's house and spend the night, and wash your feet; then you may rise early and go your way."[2] That same night, perverse men came to Lot's house and demanded him to release those two angelic beings to them so they could have sexual relations with them. Lot's response to them is heart stopping and speechless as he said, "Please, my brethren, do not do so wickedly! See now, I have two daughters who have not known a man; please, let me bring them out to you, and you may do to them as you wish; only do nothing to these men, since this is the reason they came under the shadow of my roof."[3] What? Did these demented words just come from the mouth of a father? Yes, they did!

There are two factors to point out from this shocking situation. First, Lot was willing to sacrifice and strip away the purity and the innocence of his two daughters. Second, Lot knew that those two men were angelic beings and was so religiously occupied that he was willing to destroy the fate of his two daughters in order to protect his religious beliefs of those two angelic beings,

30

by supposedly protecting them from the homosexual perverts. So, what is the point in this grim scenario? Today, like never before, we see too many individuals, especially from the younger generation, that are struggling with their sexual identity and with gender confusion. This is tragic, but the more I follow this cancerous phenomenon, the more I come to the conclusion that for the most part, it is the fault of the parent, not their son or daughter that is facing this inner identity crisis.

How did I come to this understanding? The more I hear and watch on the media where parents are boastfully supporting their five-year old, or their ten-year old, or their fifteen-year old in their decision to have their gender changed or for them to choose their sexual preference, the more this outlines how blinded, diluted, and stupid these parents have become. How in the world can a five or a ten-year-old know what their sexual preference is when they still have not fully figured out what the main purpose and function is of the primary sexual organs of their body?

Parents are there to help to guide and to remove confusion for their child rather than confuse them further. The tragic story of Lot continues. As they were escaping God's fiery judgement on Sodom and Gomorrah, his wife looked back and immediately turned into a pillar of salt. Then, after dwelling in a cave, Lot's two daughters conspired against their father and got him drunk and had incest with him, which resulted in both of them getting pregnant. You would only think that this was a movie that only Hollywood could produce, but no, this is part of our biblical history.

The chaotic story of Lot should speak loud and clear into the ears and hearts of every parent today. The demonic agenda of the Sodom and Gomorrah of today's culture is evident, but as born-again Believers, we need to see it, we need to confront it, and we need to talk about it. But if we choose to be ignorant to these crucial issues, then we shouldn't be surprised if the family unit continues to further self-destruct. Additionally, parents are the most qualified individuals and role models in the life of their child when it comes to imparting correction, knowledge, wisdom, and guidance for life (some exceptions may apply), but whenever the parent becomes absent as that Godly ordained role model and mentor to their child, then Satan will always find a substitute and those substitutes are usually destructive, toxic, and deadly.

Remember, God has not preprogrammed us with perfect decision making abilities, but He gave us a free will. You and I will make mistakes through wrongful life choices, but when God and His Word is absent in your life, then you become very vulnerable to making catastrophic or reckless choices.

Your God-given destiny for your life was designed before you were born, but it is up to you to step into that destiny.

Takeaway Lessons from the Life of Lot

- The discovery and the understanding of your identity and purpose will require a humble heart, an open mind, and a full surrender unto the Lord.
- The devil will do his best to park your kingdom purpose on an empty parking lot, but that choice is always yours to make.
- Knowing your God-given identity and purpose will give you the knowledge, the strength, and the power to resist and to fight off all sexual immorality.

9
THE IDENTITY OF ESAU
Do Not Sell Your Identity

No one is an exception to free will! God in His magnificent wisdom gave every living human being a free will and it is totally at our own discretion and utilization. In the life of Esau, we are once again reminded about the cause and effect of our free will whether for good or bad. To say that Esau made a one-time foolish mistake as it relates to his birthright would be a dire understatement. Esau's identity crisis had to do with his selfish and prideful heart.

In addition, Esau hated his brother Jacob because he stole his blessing and Esau vowed that after the death of their father, he would kill his brother.[1] This type of heart attitude does also tragically underline many Believers in the body of Christ who have hatred and jealousy for the blessings that they see in the lives of their fellow brother or sister in Christ. God gives unending blessings for everyone, but some choose to live a life of envy, jealousy, greed, and resentment. As you dive into this chapter, you will discover that your God-given identity and purpose is very valuable and consists of kingdom worth. And you will also be challenged by not placing your identity on the auction block for sale.

Your identity has a value. When you discover your identity, only then you will know what you are truly worth.

Do Not Sell Your Identity

Esau is one of those unique Bible characters who did something so foolish for the sake of simply stuffing his belly with food. We would make a dire mistake to label the fate of Esau as if God has already predestined him to sell his birthright to his younger brother Jacob. This is absolutely not so since God justly gave every human being a free will, but in regard to Esau, God has also foreseen that Esau would sell his birthright.

One tragic phenomenon that is and continues to sweep through the body of Christ is that numerous individuals are selling their God-given birthright (identity) for worldly and fleshly desires. The gospel of Matthew illustrates this point very well, "For what profit is it to a man if he gains the whole world, and loses his own soul? Or what will a man give in exchange for his soul?"[2] You see, the day you discover your potential and purpose will be the day you will take the "for sale" sign off your back. This was something that Esau was not able to do.

Esau once again outlines to us all that we are fully responsible and accountable to our God-given identity and that we need to first be very grateful that God gifted us with His kingdom potential and secondly, we need to understand how valuable this identity is. Only then will we think twice before trying to auction off our purpose and calling over some temporary pleasure or fulfilment. The life of Esau sternly teaches us that the enemy of our soul will continually try to bargain with us for our identity, just as a well-polished salesperson who would tell us that what he is offering will give us more pleasure and satisfaction.

The day you discover your potential and purpose will be the day you take the "for sale" sign off your back.

Do Not Despise Your Identity and Purpose

Chapter three in the book of Ecclesiastes shares powerful insight that there is a time for everything.[3] You only live once on this earth and not only is your earthly time limited but it is also broken down by seasons. For example, it is not recommended for a young teen girl to get pregnant since she is still maturing physically, mentally, and emotionally. And it wouldn't be wise for a farmer to sow seed in the fall or try to gather a harvest in the winter. And in like manner, our heavenly Father has divinely orchestrated specific lengths of time or seasons for our personal life and for our kingdom assignment on this earth.

In the early years, Esau had a different perspective of his birthright, but when he was extremely hungry, he allowed his fleshly appetites to despise his already predestined birthright as the firstborn. Not fully understanding the consequences of his selfish decision, we later learn that Esau cried with bitter tears begging his father to bless him. This similar portrait is seen time and time again in the lives of many, who typically in their younger years, despise their identity and purpose by exchanging it for what will satisfy them immediately instead of discovering and eventually fulfilling their kingdom assignment on this earth.

For example, if the fish is displaced out of water, it will shortly die. Why? A law was broken. The fish can only live and function when it is submerged under water. If you uproot a plant or a tree from the soil, likewise, it will wither and die. Again, a law was broken, since the roots of the plant or the tree need to be connected to the soil where they receive their needed nutrients and life. This same law is also true for you and I when it pertains to our kingdom identity and purpose on this earth. If we choose to disconnect ourselves from our true purpose on this earth, then our life begins to wither. We feel out of place, we become miserable, we experience frustration, and most of all, we feel that our life here on earth is purposeless.

Our life does not need to fall into the same pattern as Esau's life did when he was only thinking about himself at the moment that he was hungry and totally neglected to count the cost of his selfish decision. Do not despise your identity and purpose, but continually contemplate the fact that your birthright is to be a kingdom ambassador on this earth for whatever amount of time that God has already predestined for you. Additionally, here is a thought-provoking parable for you to meditate on: If your life was a bow and your purpose was the arrow, then the vital question would be, who is currently holding the bow? The lesson here is that you need to take charge of your purpose!

 You are naturally authentic when you walk in your own God-given identity.

Takeaway Lessons from the Life of Esau

- Your identity should not be forfeited because of your lack of discipline or fleshly desires.
- Your identity and purpose do have an earthly shelf life, but they should never end up on the weekend tag sale.
- Knowing your identity and purpose will challenge you to always value who you are and to be grateful for what God has entrusted you with.

10
THE IDENTITY OF JACOB
My Name Is?

E very biblical character can teach us all something unique and specific and the life of Jacob does, without a doubt, demonstrate that we cannot cheat, lie, or deceitfully discover our inner identity or our purpose on this earth. Yes, our heavenly Father has predestined our whole life, but it is up to us all to submit to His perfect will and to allow Him to bring us through every step of the way, without taking any shortcuts.

In this chapter, I will outline that there are no shortcuts to your purpose. Also, you will discover that your name has a kingdom purpose and a kingdom assignment. And finally, you will discover why it is so crucial for you to have a personal encounter with God.

The fulfillment of your kingdom assignment is not a short stroll through the park but a lifetime journey.

There Are No Shortcuts to Your Purpose

Those closest to you could become those who will challenge you to do what is wrong, just like Jacob's mother told him to deceive his father in order to get Esau's blessing. Also, you can try to masquerade yourself or disguise yourself as someone else or try to hide behind someone else's anointing or calling, but it will be a matter of time until you will be exposed.

Always remember, that there are no shortcuts to your purpose, and Jacob is a prime example to this divine principle. Throughout our whole life, we will be surrounded by individuals who have great intentions for us. This could be a parent, a spouse, a sibling, a friend, or even a pastor, but no matter who they may be, their great intentions for you will never supersede God's perfect will for your life. Too many kingdom assignments have been jeopardized or aborted simply because the individual submitted or has caved to the advice of their spouse, friend, co-worker, fellow believer, or even a parent. Again, there are no shortcuts to your purpose and no matter what great intentions others may have for you, only God truly knows who you are and what potential is embedded into your spirit man.

Your identity has a unique name and a unique purpose which you need to receive straight from the throne room of God.

Your Name Has a Kingdom Purpose and a Kingdom Assignment

Jacob's name is translated as *liar*. And throughout his life, he utilized this earthly name as a tool for his own personal gain until God met him, and they had a WWF wrestling match. On a fleshly level, Jacob was sharp, clever, and always one step ahead of others, but that only got him into further trouble. As long as Jacob was relying on his own lies and craftiness and not on God's divine purpose for his life, then each and every time Jacob would dig himself into deeper trouble.

One of the challenges in today's confused culture is that everyone has a name for you. Some call you stupid, some tell you where to go and what type of education to get, some say that you need to lie and cheat your way through the system in order to make it to the top. All of these carnal titles that bombard us on a daily basis eventually do convince many that they are just an average Bob or Suzy who have average jobs, who live average lives, who have average marriages, who make an average income, and who worship and average God.

No matter what the worldly culture dictates or what others may say about you, remember that your name has a kingdom purpose and a kingdom assignment. Whatever you allow to define you will eventually begin to give root into your heart; into your mind; and eventually into your spirit man. And whenever this occurs, you then begin to see and to value yourself in accordance to that name or description which gave root within you, but now is sprouting forth as a fruit of your daily belief system.

When you have an encounter with your Creator, you will then discover your destiny.

Why It Is So Crucial to Have a Personal Encounter with God

As you begin your personal journey of discovering your God-given identity and purpose, you will encounter a wrestling match between God and man, just like Jacob did as recorded in the book of Genesis, "For you have struggled with God and with men."[1] So, why a wrestling match between God and men? Before Jacob's supernatural encounter with God, he continually wrestled men as he would lie his way through life. And also, Jacob wrestled with God by not allowing Him to work in his heart until he had his divine encounter with God his Creator.

Sooner or later, we will all have our own personal encounter with God. One type of encounter will be because you are earnestly hungry for His presence and for discovering His perfect will for your life. The other type of encounter that you could have is when you step out of His will and by His grace, He then stands in your way to let you know that you are out of your spiritual alignment. This type of encounter is definitely the grace of God, but it could also be a very unpleasant experience since God utilizes different means in order to stop us and to bring us back into our original purpose.

Everyone's personal encounter with God will be different since God knows the best way to speak to our hearts, and he also knows that the calling and kingdom assignment of each of us on this earth is different, even though it may have certain similarities in comparison to other Believers. The life of Jacob does teach us that whenever we operate in the flesh, we hinder the Holy Spirit in revealing to us who we are and what kingdom potential abides within us, and as a result, we become more of a problem in life and in society instead of becoming a valuable asset which is able to solve the problems of others. God did not intend for His children to be taking shortcuts in order to simplify their life or to have a smooth stroll in their kingdom assignment on this earth. Absolutely not!

The less you resist the perfect will of God for your life, the more enjoyable your kingdom assignment will be.

I Will Not Let Go Unless You Bless Me

When Jacob had a supernatural encounter with God in the form of a wrestling match, God made a humorous and an intriguing statement, "And He said, 'Let me go, for day breaks.'"[2] I still have yet to hear a sound theological explanation on why God had to ask Jacob to let Him go, but it is the follow up reply from Jacob that we all need to grasp, "But he said, 'I will not let you go unless you bless me!'"[3] The response from Jacob is profound and needs to be grasped by every born-again child of God. How so? Yes, salvation was free! Yes, grace is given without measure! Yes, Jesus did absolutely everything He needed to through the death on the cross and through His resurrection! But, when it comes to discovering, understanding, and walking in our God-given kingdom identity and purpose on this earth, it is solely dependent on us.

Just because Jesus fulfilled His original purpose and now we have full access to the kingdom of God and to all of His promises in His living Word, it does not mean that everything that God has already predestined for you and I will just naturally fall into our lap. Absolutely not! Yes, Jesus fulfilled His assignment, now it is our turn to receive everything that God has in mind for us. But that will only come through prayer, fasting, walking with Him, living a holy and righteous life, and continually knocking on heaven's doors. In other words, faith without any works or any actions on our part will hinder and void out everything that God has set aside for you and I in fulfilling our kingdom assignment. We need to press into God until He blesses us.

Salvation was free, but you need to fight for your purpose.

Takeaway Lessons from the Life of Jacob

- Your identity defines who you need to become, not who you used to be.
- No matter what name, title, or description the world gives you, remember that God also has a name for you.
- You have a choice to either align yourself with the father of lies or with the Father of Truth.

11
THE IDENTITY OF JOSEPH
From the Pit to the Palace

How does one go from the pit straight into the palace? Joseph is the most qualified person to answer that question. The life, the struggles, and the journey that Joseph went through is unique in itself and the question that is so often raised is, "How does someone go from being in prison for many years straight into the palace and become the right hand of the most powerful person in the world at that time?"

To fully understand or to properly answer the above question is to once again come into agreement that whenever our heavenly Father has His hands on our life, because He has already predestined us with His kingdom assignment, we should not be surprised that a nobody could become a somebody. Once Joseph ended up in prison, I doubt that he had any human hope of getting out since his specific criminal accusation should've had him executed. But with that said, Joseph still understood that he walked before the Lord almighty and still wanted to remain faithful to Him and to the gifting that abided in him.

In this chapter, I will talk about my favorite biblical character, Joseph, who will teach us the mindset we should have when going from a prison mindset (victimhood mentality) to a palace mindset (purpose mentality). He will also teach you that your gift will make room for you. Another lesson you will learn from Joseph is that you should not allow your family or friends to hinder your purpose and to be willing to forgive those who have wronged you.

If you know your purpose, then no roadblock or barrier of life will ever deter you from your ultimate destination.

Going from a Prison Mindset to a Palace Mindset

The reason Joseph happens to be one of my favorite Bible characters is because I can easily relate to his life and his struggles. The powerful life lesson that we can take away from Joseph is not the fact that he went from rags to riches, but it can be learned as we observe his unique journey that included confusion, fear, doubt, and, most importantly, his faithfulness to God.

One of the most powerful life lessons that we can take away from Joseph is how he was continually able to have the right heart attitude in all the situations he faced. I am talking about the times when his brothers sold him, or when he was falsely accused by Potiphar's wife, or when he was in prison, or when his luck fell short with Pharaoh's butler who could've put in a good word for his possible release. It is truly remarkable knowing what Joseph went through and still maintained the right mindset. This can become a powerful guiding principle for us all. The key takeaway is that we need to change our mindset from a type of prison mindset and begin to have a palace mindset which is a mind guided by the Holy Spirit as He reveals to us our kingdom purpose and assignment on this earth, and guides us through the process.

Pride goes before a fall, but arrogance will be a snare to your purpose.

Do Not Get Arrogant or Boastful with Your God-Given Calling and Potential

Much focus has been placed on how God had predestined the path for Joseph which would ultimately lead him into the presence of Pharaoh. That is true, but I still want to point out another very important factor which we can easily neglect. Yes, Joseph was gifted by God to interpret dreams and visions, and yes God gave him two specific dreams in his early life, but Joseph got a little carried away when he began to boastfully talk about his supreme dreams to his older brothers. Do also keep in mind that he was more loved by his father Jacob, than any of his other siblings, and to make things even worse, Jacob gave him a coat of many colors. So, Joseph's physical presence was like a rainbow walking in the midst of the grey, gloomy jealousy of his brothers.

The Bible clearly warns us that pride goes before a fall[1] and that we need to always keep our heart right spiritually. Any born-again individual could easily get carried away as they begin to discover their God-given calling, and that is why it is so crucial for everyone to have at least one mentor or a spiritually mature individual who can guide you in the right direction. This is not only limited to the younger generation but also to everyone who has submitted to the perfect will of God for their personal life. I have observed both young and old who got too boastful or prideful with their calling and the end result was devastating. Likewise, I have also gone through a few of my own spiritual bumps in the road when I got carried away with my calling and potential.

Arrogance makes the individual unteachable but being boastful will set you on a path of destruction. The youthfulness of Joseph is a reflection of someone's spiritual immaturity. Spiritual immaturity is not bad, but to remain immature will result in you being arrogant or boastful.

Your purpose will not miraculously fall into your lap. You have to discover it! You have to cultivate it! And you have to release it!

Your Gift Will Make Room for You

Proverbs proclaims a powerful statement, "A man's gift makes room for him, and brings him before great men."[2] The gift in Joseph's life eventually brought him before the most powerful person in the world. As soon as Joseph interpreted Pharaoh's dream and told him what he needed to do, only then did Pharaoh know that there was no other person that was as qualified to fulfill this task as Joseph was.

In like manner, your kingdom gift will make room for you, but you need to humble yourself under the almighty hand of God. Then He will be able to use you for His kingdom purpose and in His divine timetable that He has already laid out. Remember, if you know your purpose, then no roadblocks or barriers of life will ever deter you from your ultimate destination.

With that said, here is a thought! What if Joseph willfully ignored the butler when he said that he had a distressing dream and there was no one who could interpret it? What if Joseph chose to be bitter in his heart because of his situation in the prison cell and because of this, he would have never seen the opportunity to serve the butler? No matter what, the butler would have been restored to his position anyway three days later, but also, the butler would have never advocated on Joseph's behalf before Pharaoh. And this would have kept Joseph still in the pit. The point is, do not curse or ignore those who hold the keys to your breakthrough, and while you are in a tough place, position yourself to continue to serve others. In other words, it was what Joseph did in the prison that eventually got him promoted to the palace.

Your identity is like a rare gift. Once you discover it, only then will the world have a great demand for you.

God Will Go Out of His Way

God will go out of His way and even do unthinkable things in order for us to discover our inner identity and fulfill our purpose and assignment on this earth. In the case of Joseph, God allowed Egypt and the surrounding territories to go through a severe seven-year famine for Joseph and many other individuals to be able to fulfill their purpose and assignment that God had originally engraved within their DNA.

In other words, we sometimes use too much logic to think how God will do this or how will God do that! If God desires, He will shift the nation's economy, laws, rules, regulations, and other things to prepare us or to provide for us the needed platform to discover our identity and to fulfill our kingdom purpose on this earth.

Again, the key person that played a vital role in Joseph's acceleration and fulfillment of his purpose was the butler who was imprisoned by Pharaoh. That is why Joseph needed to end up in a prison cell to meet this butler who would eventually present him before Pharaoh. Let us take a quick look at how God works in very unorthodox ways:

- God used Joseph's brothers to sell him to Midianite traders.
- God used the traders to sell Joseph to Potiphar.
- God used Potiphar's immoral wife to have Joseph imprisoned.
- God gave favor to Joseph before the prison warden who gave Joseph the freedom and liberty to serve other jailers.
- God gave the baker and the butler prophetic dreams, which Joseph interpreted.
- God gave Pharaoh two troubling dreams.
- And finally, the butler remembered Joseph and told Pharaoh that he knew a man that could help interpret the king's dreams.

God will go out of His way, not because He has to, but because He loves you so much. The above outline of Joseph's journey towards fully walking into his kingdom calling is fascinating, but I highly doubt that he personally enjoyed the process. Remember, no matter what process or season you may go through, God is always in full control over your life.

43

Family and friends are resourceful tools to fulfilling your kingdom assignment but could also become weapons of hinderance.

Do Not Allow Your Family and Friends to Hinder Your Purpose and Passion

The sad truth is that often family members tend to be one of the greatest purpose and passion killers in your life and in a similar manner, so are close friends. In the life of Joseph, when he shared his heart's purpose and passion, his brothers ridiculed him and got angry with him and in like manner, so was his father upset with Joseph.

Often, parents make a grave mistake in regard to their child's identity and purpose from God because the parent does not fully understand or comprehend what gifts, calling, and potential God has placed within their child. So, as the child begins to discover their identity and purpose and share it with their parents or siblings or friends, often the response is not always positive. The challenge for us all is not to allow our family members or our friends to hinder our purpose and passion.

Knowing your identity will allow you to bury your past and give birth to your future.

Knowing Your Identity and Purpose Will Give You the Ability and the Power to Forgive

Some of the greatest painful offenses come from within your own family. And Joseph is a personified example of this. To forgive your offender or accuser is not easy, especially when people treat you like dirt, use or abuse you, and chew you up and eventually spit you out. Forgiveness is always a personal choice, and whether you choose to forgive or not will determine on how successfully you will be able to function in your kingdom purpose.

Many born-again Believers have aborted their kingdom assignment on this earth simply because they were not able to forgive others for the wrongdoing or the pain that they have caused them. What is unforgiveness? Unforgiveness is like a self-made prison cell that you lock yourself into and throw away the key. When Joseph's brothers bowed before him, he recognized that they were his brothers. At that moment, he could have allowed anger and bitterness to take hold of his heart which would have resulted in their imprisonment, but Joseph had compassion for his brothers and stepped aside and wept instead. Because Joseph fully understood his kingdom purpose, he eventually spoke these profound words to his brothers, "Do not be afraid, for *am* I in the place of God? But as for you, you meant evil against me; but God meant it for good, in order to bring it about as it is this day, to save many people alive."[3]

Knowing your identity and purpose will give you the ability and the power to forgive those who hurt or wrong you on any scale. And only those who choose to take the path of forgiveness will be those same individuals who will be able to fully walk and function in their kingdom assignment. Remember, no matter how horrific or unpleasant your life journey may be, just continue to trust in the Lord and He will eventually bring you from the pit and into the palace.

Knowing your purpose will transition your pit-mindset into kingdom thinking.

Takeaway Lessons from the Life of Joseph

- Your identity will make you stand out from the rest of the crowd.
- Your identity and purpose will take you through a specific path of development and maturity, which will not always be pleasant.
- Your kingdom assignment is always bigger than you, so you need to fully rely on a big God who knows exactly what He is doing.

12
THE IDENTITY OF AMRAM AND JOCHEBED
The Power and Purpose of Parental Mentorship

D avid is a name that we all know! Jonah, we learned about from our Sunday school teacher! And yes, the virgin Mary was the mother of Jesus! But who in the world is Amram and Jochebed?

Amram and Jochebed were the biological parents of Moses and the Bible only shares a small handful of verses that pertain to them. But what little may have been spoken about them does speak volumes as it relates to their son Moses who became a powerful leader, spiritual advisor, and the first pastor of the largest megachurch.

Also, what makes the story of Moses so unique, is how his mother, Jochebed, preserved his life. She first hid him for three months and then made a basket out of papyrus reeds and covered it with tar, so it would be waterproof, and then sent it down the river where the daughter of Pharaoh found it.[1] This brave act was a suicide attempt, since Pharaoh had ordered for all male born children to be thrown into the river.[2]

The purpose of Moses could not have been fulfilled on this earth if Moses' parents would not have trusted the Lord and acted out in much boldness, when they saw something special in this precious little child. Moses' parents became yielded tools in the hand of God. And in this short chapter, you will take away a better understanding of the power and purpose of parental mentorship, and why parents play a very vital role in the life of their child.

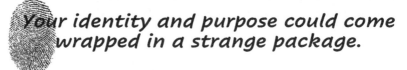

Your identity and purpose could come wrapped in a strange package.

The Power and Purpose of Parental Mentorship

Being a parent of three, my eldest already a sophomore in High school, does keep you on your toes. Also, having served as a youth pastor for many years and witnessing much destruction and confusion taking place in the lives of teenagers has provided me with much valuable insight for raising and disciplining my own children. This by no means automatically makes me the most qualified and knowledgeable parent as it relates to raising my children. Absolutely not! But, all of those valuable years have sketched out for me the understanding that I play a vital role as a parent and am a mentor to my own children.

Even though the names of Amram and Jochebed are barely spoken of behind the pulpits or in Sunday school settings, this still does not undermine the important role that they both fulfilled in the life of their son Moses. This is actually one of the key gems that we as parents need to grasp from the life and the deeds of Moses' parents. In the book of Exodus, the New Living Translation points out an important aspect about the birth of Moses, "The woman became pregnant and gave birth to a son. She saw that he was a special baby and kept him hidden for three months."[3] Jochebed, saw that her son Moses was no ordinary baby, but a *special baby.*

This is a powerful point for every parent to grasp. Each and every child that our heavenly Father has blessed us with is special and not ordinary. When we allow the Holy Spirit to reveal to us that our son or daughter possesses a kingdom imprint and that they have a kingdom assignment on their life, we then begin to protect them from the worldly system and ideology, just like Moses' parents protected him from being killed.

Of course, as parents, we are very limited and need to heavily rely on the guidance of the Holy Spirit and on the fundamental building blocks of the Word of God which will become the unshakable foundation for our children. And as we rely on God's Word and on the guidance of the Holy Spirit, we then will be able to have the necessary wisdom, knowledge, discernment, and revelation as it relates to our child. And as we become that much needed mentor and life coach to our child, God will be able to use us as a tool to shape the heart and mind of our child and to direct them into their divine kingdom assignment and purpose.

Mentorship or parental mentoring is in excessive deficit in our current society. On the most part, it is because some do not see the need for mentorship and on the other spectrum, our society is struggling with broken families and with broken marriages. The child or the children automatically become the victims to this decay in the family unit. One powerful truth that all of us need to grasp is that whatever you were born to do on this earth, the ability to do it is already built within you! God has entrusted each and every parent to help their child discover and understand what kingdom gift, talent, and potential is hidden within them. So, what does mentorship look like? And why does a parent or parents play a crucial role in mentoring? Let us look at the illustration of the power and the purpose of mentorship:

- On the outside, we see a tree, but hidden within is furniture, houses, towns, and cities.
- On the outside we see rugged looking granite and marble rocks, but hidden within are fancy countertops, statues and monuments, and massive buildings & structures.
- On the outside we see black and nasty looking liquid but hidden within is fuel and gasoline.
- On the outside we see a rough looking stone, but hidden within is a diamond, an emerald, a ruby, or a pearl.

In like manner, we as parents could see just a little innocent child on the outside, or a rebellious teenager, or a lost and confused young adult, but hidden within them is untapped kingdom potential. It is in the form of a purpose that needs to be discovered and released so that the whole world can benefit from what God has originally engraved into your child's spiritual DNA.

Additionally, I want to encourage every parent, young or old, single or married, that God has a phenomenal plan for your son or daughter and none of us will ever know in the early years if our child could be the next Moses whom the Lord will use in a mighty way to transform a culture or to transform a nation and influence the lives of millions. Stay focused on the living Word of God, rely on the Holy Spirit, and entrust your child or children into the hands of the almighty God.

Your purpose cannot be fulfilled or accomplished by yourself, it will always require the help, the guidance, the wisdom, and the mentorship of others around you.

Takeaway Lessons from the Life of Amram and Jochebed

- Do not oppose or resist the guidance of your parent since God will use them to guide you towards your kingdom assignment.
- If you truly desire to fulfill your kingdom purpose, then you need to honor, respect, and submit to the mentorship of others.
- Your identity and purpose will attract to and connect you with specific individuals who will become your mentors or life coaches.

13
THE IDENTITY OF MOSES
Called for Greatness

oses is recognized as the first pastor in the Bible and in the Christian faith. It is estimated that he had a congregation of more than two million. His church was a portable tent, and his leaders were a bunch of complaining troublemakers. Not only that, but the book of Numbers records numerous occasions where God killed thousands of Israelites because of their complaining or rebellion.

I believe if every pastor carefully and sincerely read through the life of Moses and what he had to deal with during those forty years in the wilderness, then I am more than sure that these pastors would think that their congregants and staff is the best in the whole world. You see, the identity of Moses is very special, because he was the least qualified person for this job, but that still did not stop God from using him. Why? Because he was called for greatness.

As you journey through the life of Moses, you will discover that your purpose may have humble beginnings, but eventually it will lead you to greatness. And you will also understand that fear is the enemy to your kingdom assignment. Also, you will see that your identity will require proper growth and maturity. And finally, you will be challenged with the question, "What are you holding in your hands?"

Your kingdom assignment will always start off small, quiet, and unseen, but will eventually lead you to greatness.

Your Purpose May Have Humble Beginnings but Eventually It Will Lead You to Greatness

Who would have ever thought that a persecuted baby would one day grow up in the palace of the same Pharaoh that placed a death mark over him and all male children under the age of two? God does have a sense of humor! This boy,

Moses, grew up as spoiled royalty, having absolutely everything he would desire, until one day compassion and conviction began to bother him as he saw the Israelites being heavily abused by the Egyptians. This was the beginning of self-discovery of his identity and assignment, but he had no knowledge of what that assignment was. Eventually, one day, he killed an Egyptian, which resulted in his excommunication from the land.

As Moses hid himself in the land of Midian for forty years, he thought that this is how it should be until he had his fiery encounter with the Almighty God. Let us analyze some details of what occurred during the burning bush experience, and take a look at what excuses Moses gave to God, which are no different than what excuses you and I give to God:

- God gives Moses the shortest introduction of who He is, "I am the God of your father."[1]
- God seriously cuts to the chase and gives Moses a serious assignment.
- Moses' "book of excuses":
  - "Who am I that I should go to Pharaoh and that I should bring the children of Israel out of Egypt?"
  - "What will I say to your people if they ask me who sent you?"
  - "What shall I call You?"
  - "What if the people do not believe me?"
  - "What if the people will not listen to me?"
  - "I cannot talk well, and my speech is slow?"
  - "Lord, please send someone else!"
- After Moses final excuse, God became very angry with him.

Excuses originate from fear, but fear is generated from not knowing your identity and purpose. Not knowing your identity and purpose will generate a whole new batch of excuses. You see, your purpose may have humble beginnings, but eventually it will lead you to greatness. Sure, you may have been born out of wedlock, or as an orphan, or in a broken family, or with some kind of birth defects, or in extreme poverty, but that should never become a reason for God not to use you for His kingdom purpose. So, whatever your humble beginnings may be, always know that God is much more interested in you fulfilling His purpose on this earth than you will ever be.

Fear is fueled from your lack of trust in God's perfect will for your life.

Fear Is the Enemy of Your Kingdom Assignment

Moses tried to reason with the Lord that he could not speak well and that the Israelites would not listen to him and that he was also not qualified for this assignment. This resulted in the Lord getting angry at him. Fear may not be anything new but fear still continues to be the enemy of everyone's kingdom assignment.

The fear of public speaking is still considered one of the most common fears today. And as soon as the enemy of your soul discovers your kingdom assignment, he will do whatever he can to fill your heart, your mind, and your feelings with fear and intimidation. Why? Because he knows that if he is successful, then you will not fully function or be able to fulfill your kingdom assignment and you will always be full of excuses.

Fear is a deadly tool that the devil will use against you, since fear has the power to paralyze your faith, your passion, your vision, and the desire to fulfill your kingdom assignment. But Timothy reminds us with these encouraging words, "For God has not given us a spirit of fear, but of power and of love and of a sound mind."[2] Fear may be a natural human characteristic, but fear should never become your excuse for not fulfilling your kingdom assignment.

Do not allow your future grave to rob this world or the next generation of the hidden potential that abides within you.

You Plan but the Lord Will Direct

Our heavenly Father, through His divine grace, reveals our future through His Word, through prophecy, through dreams and visions, and through spiritual impartation of the Holy Spirit. This is all great, but God also in His divine wisdom does not tell us the exact route that we need to take or show us all of the obstacles and roadblocks that we will encounter on the way to our destination. This was exactly what occurred with Moses and the Israelites.

The Book of Proverbs records, "A man's heart plans his way, but the Lord directs his steps."[3] This was definitely evident in the life of Moses where God was fully orchestrating every step of the way from his birth, and all the way to his death. I wholeheartedly believe that God gives us the desires of our heart and also gives us the opportunity to make plans for our life. God will never force you to marry a specific individual or work for a specific company

51

or live in a specific geographical location. We have the freedom to make all of the above choices and decisions, but we also need to fully trust the Lord to direct our every step, so we are not placing our trust upon our knowledge, wisdom, or personal ego. Yes, you have the free will to plan, but you also need to trust in the Lord as He directs your steps.

Identity always abides by the law of the seed, which will require time for the necessary growth.

Your Identity Will Require Proper Growth and Maturity

Moses, troubled by the Egyptian who was mistreating a Jewish slave, killed that Egyptian. Yes, God did predestine Moses to be the deliverer of Israel, but God had His own way plan to deal with the Egyptians. If Moses continued to kill one or two Egyptians per day, he would need to live for a thousand years in order to kill as many as God has killed in one night and in one water baptism of the Red Sea. In other words, Moses tried to operate and function in his purpose forty years too early.

You should never rush your purpose! You should not try to be ahead of God! And you should patiently wait upon the Lord because His timing and His seasons for your life are divine and perfect! Our heavenly Father, in His endless wisdom, has already orchestrated everything perfectly. And all He needs to know is if we are willing to submit under His almighty hand as He executes His kingdom purpose on this earth, by using us as one of His tools. Your kingdom identity will require proper growth and maturity, and only the Lord will truly know when you are ready.

Your identity may seem awkward in the beginning, but as time goes by you will discover its full potential.

What Are You Holding in Your Hands?

After Moses gave every possible excuse from the "book of excuses" on why he was not qualified or why he did not possess the necessary credentials for God to use him, God asked Moses a powerful question in response: "What is that in your hand?"[4] This is the exact same question that our heavenly Father is asking every individual who comes before Him with a mouthful of excuses.

If all you see is a stick in your hand, then just stick around with the Lord and watch what He does with your simple stick, which He gave to you. Our issue, just likes Moses' issue, is that we only see a stick, but God sees what that stick can do. We see our limitations, but God sees untapped potential that is lying dormant within us. And we oftentimes see manmade limitations that have been placed on us by others, but God sees a divine human being with a unique potential that needs to become a kingdom ambassador on this earth.

Right now, you may think that what your holding in your hand is an insignificant piece of wood, but God wants to let you know that this so-called insignificant stick can do supernatural things. This stick is your kingdom assignment, potential, purpose, talent, skills, and abilities that God has engraved into your spiritual DNA. What you and I need to do is just ask ourselves an honest question: What am I holding in my hand? And then we should allow the Holy Spirit to provide for us the answer to that question! The answer could also come through dreams, visions, prophecy, various situations, opportunities, or individuals, as the Lord never limits Himself on how He helps you and I answer that question.

Just because you do not know or do not understand or still have not discovered what tools or what potential God has bestowed upon you does not mean it is not there. Many times Christians become discouraged and frustrated in the process of trying to discover and understand what they are holding in their hands, and as a result, they just cast aside their stick or their calling and live a life of mediocrity. When this occurs, in the process of time, these same individuals begin to grow in anger and bitterness towards God thinking that God is not interested in using them or that God has not equipped their life with any kingdom significance.

The life journey of Moses is truly remarkable and a very lengthy journey to follow. But it is also full of adventures and supernatural occurrences. In the same manner, God desires for our life on this earth to be adventurous and exciting, but we also need to have plenty of patience. And we also need to have the revelation that we were born for greatness.

You will never be able to successfully influence others until you discover your identity and purpose.

Passing the Baton

I am very passionate when it comes to the subject of mentoring or mentorship. And I believe that this is one of the weakest links in the body of Christ. If we carefully follow the story of Moses, we see a handful of references where he took Joshua with him to the mountain of the Lord, and as Moses was in intimate fellowship with the almighty God, Joshua stayed on the mountain waiting for him. And there were a couple of times where Moses was in the presence of God for forty days and yes, Joshua waited for him.

As the ministry and the mission of Moses came to an end, we read the following, "Now Joshua the son of Nun was full of the spirit of wisdom, for Moses had laid his hands on him; so the children of Israel heeded him, and did as the Lord had commanded Moses."[4] The key takeaway here is for us to grasp the importance of passing the baton to the next individual or to the next generation. Today, the body of Christ is still struggling with the sickness of too many pastors or leaders still holding onto their baton. Passing the baton is a sign of health but holding onto the baton is a sign of spiritual sickness!

Knowing your purpose will prepare your heart and mind for raising the next generation of leaders.

Takeaway Lessons from the Life of Moses

- Your identity will always have a unique beginning from the days of your childhood.
- Your God-given identity and purpose will stir up your heart and spirit man every time you see, hear, or encounter something that is connected to your kingdom assignment on this earth.
- Never despise, ridicule, or complain about your kingdom purpose while it is in the early stages of maturity.

14
THE IDENTITY OF JOSHUA AND CALEB
Taking Hold of God's Promises

The Bible only records two individuals who were part of the rebellious generation that went into the Promised Land. That was Joshua and Caleb! These were the only two spies that came back to Moses with a great report about the potential of the Promised Land.

The story of Joshua and Caleb teaches us powerful life principles of patience, of waiting upon the Lord, and of holding onto God's promises. They both literally had to wait for forty years before they could step into the land that was flowing with milk and honey. Often, we cannot even handle a few months before we start to moan and complain to God about our uncomfortable situation or an agonizing season.

When the spies came back with the negative report, together with the Israelites they began to complain to Moses about the giants in the Promised Land, but at that moment, Joshua and Caleb tore their clothes and began to plead with the Israelites to realize that God would fight on their behalf. But the whole congregation wanted to stone them for their beliefs and for their stance. And here is another powerful truth to behold, that there will be some who are willing to cast you out, harshly oppose you, or even try to bring harm upon you, because of the inner convictions that you possess that are contrary to the masses.

The identity of Joshua and Caleb sheds a lot of light for us all as we learn to place less blame on people or circumstances and begin to trust the Lord to bring our purpose and calling to fruition. Also, the Bible records that Caleb was eighty-five years old when he asked Joshua to give him the mountain that he originally saw forty years previously, so that he could claim it as an inheritance. Caleb said these profound words, "As yet I *am* strong this day as on the day that Moses sent me; just as my strength *was* then, so now is my strength for war, both for going out and for coming in."[1] Joshua did bless him and he eventually took that mountain as an old man.

In this particular chapter, I want to outline two primary factors that we can learn from Joshua and Caleb. First, the importance of knowing and understanding that time will never be our friend, so we need to patiently wait upon the Lord, since He knows exactly what He is doing. Secondly, you will also grasp the importance of why your kingdom identity needs to manifest in your family. Both of these factors are crucial for you to behold.

Your identity is like a GPS that is meant to keep you on the right track towards your final destination.

Sometimes the Preparation for Your Assignment Could Take Many Years

Joshua and Caleb waited forty-years before they officially stepped into the Promised Land. Yes, patience does pay off, if only you trust the Lord in the process. One thing that continually amazes me is that the Word of God is full of plenty of examples and illustrations that can give us plenty of guidance, insight, support, revelations, and wisdom as it relates to discovering and understanding our kingdom assignment on this earth.

We plan for months or sometimes a few years for our next family vacation. The preparation for your wedding day also takes a while and entails many details. Even pregnancies demand a nine-month period before the couple is able to see and enjoy the fruit of their love. So, the truthful fact is that sometimes the preparation for your kingdom assignment could take many years.

As we carefully observe the life of Joshua and Caleb, we can honestly see that it was not their own doing that thrust them back into the wilderness for 40 more years. And their significance teaches us all a powerful lesson when it comes to trusting the Lord no matter what.

Your family, your marriage, your spouse, or your children all play a vital role in you fulfilling your kingdom assignment.

Your Kingdom Identity Needs to Manifest in Your Family Life

Family values and principles are very crucial in a believer's life, and one of the most powerful examples of this was conveyed through the mouth of Joshua, "Choose for yourself this day whom you will serve; But as for me and my house, we will serve the Lord."[2]

Knowing your identity in Christ as a parent, or as a husband, or as a wife is the key to a successful marriage, and it is a key to a blessed family life. When you know that God is the center of your family and His Word is your foundation, then you can have the assurance that everything will be well. This does not mean that you will not face many uncomfortable seasons or tough situations, but no matter how dire a family issue you may face, you can always rely upon the Lord to bring you through it. Why? Because He has a great purpose for you, and the last thing He wants for any of His children is for them to remain in the wilderness of their problems for the rest of their lives.

The life examples of Joshua and Caleb are just another reminder that we need to place our trust in the Lord's timing and that our family, our marriage, and our children are part of your identity and destiny. If the family unit is broken, out of alignment, or unhealthy, then it will be difficult and even impossible for you to fulfill your kingdom mission on this earth.

The more you grab ahold of God's promises for your life, the more you will understand your calling and purpose on this earth.

Takeaway Lessons from the Life of Joshua and Caleb

- Discovering or understanding your identity and purpose is not an overnight event, but that will require time and plenty of patience.
- Whether you are married or not, family plays a very essential role in shaping, fine tuning, and in helping you to function in your kingdom calling.
- Do not abort your purpose and assignment on this earth just because God does not operate to your standards or to your timetable.

15
THE IDENTITY OF RAHAB
God Does Have a Sense of Humor

There is a strategic reason why I subtitled this chapter, "God Does Have A Sense of Humor!" Our God is a glorious and a majestic God, but He also does things that will never make sense to our human logic. In the first chapter of the gospel of Matthew it talks about the genealogy of Jesus, and yes, Rahab the harlot is part of that genealogy. That is why God does have a sense of humor.

Yes, Rahab was a prostitute and a Gentile heathen, but she was not ignorant about who the Israelites were and how powerful their God was. When she chose to hide the two Israeli spies, she entered an agreement with them that if she protected them that they would not destroy her or her household once the Israelites attacked Jericho. Eventually, that is exactly what occurred. Rahab's whole family gathered in her place and when the Jericho walls came crashing down and every human being in the city was killed, Rahab, her parents and her siblings were the only ones who were spared.

The story of Rahab is truly astounding, and shows us that God can take even a prostitute and use her as a powerful testimony of how God can literally turn anyone's life around. You will uncover in this chapter that God is full of surprises, and that He is able to take someone that is considered an outcast or the scum of society and turn them into an ambassador for His kingdom.

Your purpose was uniquely designed by God to solve a specific problem on this earth.

God's Purpose for Your Life Will Surprise and Shock Many Individuals

Who would have ever thought that Rahab the prostitute would become part of the genealogy of the Son of God? But she did! In like manner, many people always ask the age-old question: How could God ever use a person like me? But He can! And He is also eagerly looking forward to it!

When you have discovered your identity and purpose, people's opinions of who you are will no longer matter. I could only image what kind of reputation Rahab had amongst her own people, but when a divine moment came knocking on her door, she opened the door and her whole life was forever changed. And after everyone in her city was killed, all of their opinions of Rahab perished with them.

You see, eagles excel in flight, fish excel in swimming, cheetahs excel in running, and lions excel in hunting! So, it is imperative for you to discover your gift, to grow in your gift, and to excel in your gift. Who would have ever thought that someone like Rahab would be considered as a biblical icon, and someone to be engraved into the genealogy of Jesus? Just like many of us are shocked and awed by the historical significance that Rahab's role played in history, likewise many will become surprised and shocked to learn that God can take a nobody like you and I and make us part of His genealogy as well as part of His kingdom plan.

Your divine identity has the ability and the power to transform you from who you were into who you need to become.

Do Not Allow the World to Prostitute Your Identity and Purpose

The word *prostitute* is defined as: betrayer, cheater, deceiver, and seducer.[1] All of the above outline the characteristics of the devil. The world and the ruler of this worldly system desires to prostitute your identity and purpose. You see, Rahab lived her life as a prostitute, but she internally recognized that these two spies were no ordinary individuals just looking for a goodtime. And she risked her own life in order to save theirs. But in doing so, she also understood that the God of Israel was an Almighty God who had destroyed all of the enemies of the Israelites. Because she recognized this truth, it was this same truth that eventually saved her and her whole household.

Most, if not all who are reading this book may not have a lifestyle of a prostitute, but absolutely all of us are bombarded by the devil and this worldly system that is trying to deceive, seduce, and cause us to stray away from the will of God for our personal life. Do not allow the world or its demonic system to prostitute your identity and purpose on this earth. The story of Rahab the harlot is not only solely unique to her, but it also speaks volumes to us all. The devil knows that if he is able to prostitute your identity, then you will end up naked, broken, insecure, and full of fear. This was exactly how Adam and Eve felt when they allowed the serpent to deceive them.

Our heavenly Father, through His Son Jesus, has stripped away any and every worldly title, description, or accusation that likened us to heavy, nasty, and ugly garments, and instead He gave us a white robe of righteousness, holiness, and purity. And the best part of it all is that we are also called His bride.

The identity of Rahab is truly profound, and her lifestyle should be an encouragement to all, especially to those who feel that they are an outcast or neglected by the society. God does not and will never have any outcasts. No human being is ever second-hand in His eyes. You truly are a masterpiece and your name is part of God's ultimate genealogy, if only you chose to believe that and receive it into your spirit man. And remember, God's sense of humor is evident when He takes a wretched nobody like you and I and makes us His children and His kingdom ambassadors.

Your heavenly Father has embedded adventure, creativity, and excitement, into your identity and purpose.

Takeaway Lessons from the Life of Rahab

- You should never allow your past life, or your past lifestyle, to make you into an outcast once God transforms your whole life.
- Your identity and kingdom calling will surprise and shock many, especially those who knew you before you became born-again.
- Your divine identity and purpose have tremendous value and worth, so do not sell it or prostitute it.

16
THE IDENTITY OF GIDEON
Lord, Are You Sure You Have the Right Person?

T he story of Gideon and his three hundred valiant men sounds like a good folk tale because Gideon himself was insecure and afraid. John C. Maxwell once stated, "Who you are determines the way you see everything and everyone. You cannot separate your identity from your perspective." The perspective that Gideon had of himself in the beginning resembled the absence of his God-given identity, and that is why he was initially feeble, fearful, and full of doubts.

The life story of Gideon should be very encouraging and motivational to every believer, because when he had his first encounter with the Angel of the Lord,[1] Gideon did not know his kingdom identity or his assignment on this earth. This does resemble every born-again believer, but why? When we first give our life to the Lord, we just know the fundamentals: that we are saved and forgiven, and if we die right now, then we will go to heaven. This is all true, but there is a lot more to this and as you move forward throughout this chapter, you will discover through the life and the identity of Gideon that you do possess kingdom power and you can cast aside all fear, doubt, or intimidations.

Your identity may look small to you, but it is mighty and powerful in the eyes of God.

Your Identity and Purpose Is Mighty and Powerful

The Lord in His opening conversation addressed Gideon as *mighty man of valor*, which probably intimidated him. With that said, we can also be very intimidated when we read through the living Word of God and discover everything that our heavenly Father says about us and what potential and purpose we all possess. For example:

- "Whatever you bind on earth will be bound in heaven, and whatever you loose on earth will be loosed in heaven."[2]
- "And the Lord will make you the head and not the tail; you shall be above only, and not be beneath."[3]
- "But you are a chosen generation, a royal priesthood, a holy nation, His own special people, that you may proclaim the praises of Him who called you out of darkness into His marvelous light."[4]

Your identity and kingdom assignment on this earth is mighty and powerful which will give you favor before others and make you very influential. The challenge for us all is to simply believe in the Word of God and in His promises that He has already predestined. And it is essential that we continually abide in His Word as it will nourish our hearts and provide the needed revelation to who we are and what potential abides within us.

The more you doubt your purpose and calling, the more disqualified you will become in your excuses to not do what God has anointed you to do.

The Book of Doubt and Excuses

Every living human being possesses a personal book that I call "the book of doubt and excuses," and Gideon provides us with a little taste of his own book. Let us take a look at the dialogue Gideon had with God:[5]

> God: *"The Lord is with you, you mighty man of valor."*
> Gideon: *"If the Lord is with us, then why has all this happened to us?"*
> God: *"Go in this might of yours and you shall save Israel."*
> Gideon: *"How can I save Israel, my clan is the weakest. And I'm the least in my father's house."*
> God: *"Surely I will be with you and you will defeat the Midianites as one man."*
> Gideon: *"If I found favor in your sight, then show me a sign that it is you who talk with me."*

Gideons pathetic dialogue continued further, but God was very patient with him, just as much as He is very patient with all of us. What we learn is that Gideon was insecure, full of fear, cautious, undecisive, and had low self-esteem. His lack of everything does resemble many Believers today. We allow our fear and insecurities to get the best of us and this often affects our faith, which results in losing trust in our heavenly Father and in the promises that He has for us. Remember, without faith we cannot please God and without faith we cannot fully function in our kingdom assignment. And for as long as we feel afraid or insecure, we will continually doubt the promises, the blessings, and the kingdom assignment that God has for us. The challenge for you and I is to tear up our "book of excuses," and turn to God's Word which is full of His promises for His children.

God never makes mistakes, and that is why your kingdom calling was strategically orchestrated by God.

Takeaway Lessons from the Life of Gideon

- Until you allow the Holy Spirit to reveal to you your God-given identity and purpose, you will continually question whether God has a specific kingdom assignment for you or whether you are qualified enough to do it.
- Your identity and purpose will never be accurately valued in accordance to human standards, and you and I can only discover our true value and worth from our Creator.
- Doubt, fear, intimidation, and procrastination originate from the "book of excuses," while boldness, determination, faith, and hope are derived from the Word of God.

17
THE IDENTITY OF SAMSON
Sleeping with Your Enemy

There is a reason why Samson tends to be one of the favorite Bible characters for children! Before the fame and the world-wide recognition of Arnold Schwarzenegger, Samson was the first Mr. Universe. The life and the calling of Samson were special as his parents received specific instructions from the angel of the Lord on how he needed to be raised and groomed for the Lord's specific assignment.

The story and the life of Samson is very unique, and in this scenario, God specifically chose something that basically carries no spiritual or theological connotations, but only involved physical strength. Why is this factor so crucial to comprehend? I grew up in a traditional and a conservative environment that most, if not all of the time, placed emphasis on spiritual things or strictly limited ministry to church, evangelism, or missions. I never knew that God could use my physical body, or my intellect, or my entrepreneur skills for His kingdom purpose. Samson is a powerful example that God is creative, unlimited, and has given specific gifts for a specific purpose. The Apostle Paul outlined in 1 Corinthians 12 that we all have diversities of gifts, which is for the profit of all.[1]

In addition, what makes the life and the story of Samson of great importance is his parents, particularly his mother who had been barren. When the Angel of the Lord appeared to Samson's mother, he told her that she would conceive a son, and the Angel also directed her to strictly refrain from eating anything unclean or from drinking wine or any similar drink, because her son would become a Nazirite. In other words, his mother needed to restrain herself from certain fleshly appetites, which showed a type of devotion and consecration unto the Lord. This positioned her as a vital tool in the hands of God who would use her in raising and grooming her son Samson to fulfill his identity. This truth also pertains to single mothers who choose to devote their life to the almighty God and submit their life into His hand. And by doing so, He would use them powerfully in the life of their child or children.

In this chapter, as we analyze the life of Samson, you will discover the uniqueness of his gift which should bring much clarity to the uniqueness of your own God-given gift. And you will also understand some of Samson's struggles and challenges that he faced in his life. And you will see that the struggles he was faced with are no different than those that we are also faced with as we strive to live a life of purity and faithfulness to our kingdom assignment on this earth.

Your kingdom purpose has enormous potential, but it solely depends on you and on how much you allow your purpose to be released.

The Bigger the Tree, the Harder They Fall

It has been said, "The higher the climb, the greater the fall." But if that is the case, should we all avoid reaching greater heights in our personal life? Should we just remain average for the rest of our life? Absolutely not!

In the case of the mighty macho-man, Samson, yes, he was the strongest and the most feared man of his time, but like anyone else, he also had his own weaknesses. Is it possible to become great, successful, and very influential? Yes! And will that automatically qualify me for a great fall? No! But like any human being, everyone is full of weaknesses, and absolutely no one is exempt from falling to the bottom from their sky-scraper status.

Yes, the bigger the tree, the harder they will fall, but this has also been one of the greatest soundbites in the body of Christ. Often I have heard fellow Believers with much humility who would typically say, "Be careful not to excel or become too successful or else the devil will break you into many pieces." The truth is that God wants us all to mature to our fullest kingdom potential, so we can become the much-needed vessel in His divine hands. Just as no one would want to buy a new car with two wheels or with half an engine, God does not want half of our potential but the whole thing. And whenever you discover or understand your potential, you should never be afraid or intimidated by its magnitude since it is God who distributes to each one as He wills, not as we choose.

Your spiritual DNA will not always reflect in the physical realm as it does in the spiritual realm.

65

A Theological Dilemma

As of today, every movie that was ever made about the character of Samson always portrayed him as a macho man with muscular physique, which was typically depicted by a body builder. And yes, my Sunday school teacher shared plenty of Samson stories of this muscular Bible hero. But I want to challenge you to consider a different perspective, that there is no biblical reference stating that Samson was very muscular or had a huge physical appearance. Ponder on this for a minute!

With that said, could it be that Samson looked like an average Joe without the appearance of Arnold Schwarzenegger's body? And this also could be a justifiable understanding to why the average person, or the Philistines were not intimidated by Samson. When Goliath stood before the Israelites and mocked them for forty-days, no soldier dared to fight him, because he was a massive looking monster who could crush a man's skull with his bare hands. But on the contrary, I personally believe that Samson was just a scrawny looking guy! And this again shows God's great sense of humor as we witness often throughout the whole Bible.

Remember, God once challenged the prophet Samuel with these powerful words when he came to anoint the next king over Israel, "Do not look at his appearance or at his physical stature, because I have refused him. For *the Lord does* not *see* as man sees; for man looks at the outward appearance, but the Lord looks at the heart."[2] This is also true today, we often tend to put too much emphasis on specific things as Believers, and in the process, neglect ourselves. Or we even despise our fellow man.

Just as we may have taken the mighty Samson appearing as an epiphany of Mr. Universe out of context, in like manner we often do not see our self or others as God sees us. This is critical for us all to comprehend. Why? Because too many Believers have become victims to someone else's description of who they think you ought to be, and sadly, much of this demoralization comes from within the body of Christ.

The *theological dilemma* about having this perspective in our own lives comes when we believe man's interpretation of who God made us to be on this earth, instead of allowing the Word of God and the Holy Spirit to reveal His divine plan for us. Samson might have looked too ordinary, but when he operated in his gifting and purpose, then everyone feared him or gave glory to God. This is also true for all of us! Before the eyes of others, we seem ordinary, but when we begin to operate or to release our kingdom potential, then our ambassadorship and influence becomes evident and established before others.

Your God-given uniqueness will make some people glad and supportive, while others will roll their eyes and simply shake their head.

Your Uniqueness May Look Like an Insignificant Jawbone

Nowhere before or after was a military story recorded of someone killing a thousand soldiers with a jawbone! And in order for anyone to acknowledge the credibility of such a story does require faith. I highly doubt that those Philistine soldiers charged at Samson with their bare fists. Absolute not! They were fully armed for warfare and utilized everything in their arsenal. And to make this unique situation more mesmerizing is the fact that Samson did not hold on to this useful jawbone. After he was finished with it, he threw it away.

Often, our uniqueness may look like an insignificant jawbone, which seems purposeless until the opportune moment comes. And this insignificance turns into something magnificent as the anointing of the Lord begins to operate in you and through you. Just as Samson was not fretting that he did not have a sword, a shield, or a spear available to him can also be true for all of us. Yes, God has equipped us with all necessary tools and resources to fulfill our kingdom assignment on this earth, and God will not leave us naked or hopeless in the moment of opportunity when we can glorify His name through our calling on this earth.

Additionally, there is one more powerful fact to consider. When Samson's anger was aroused against his father-in-law who gave his betrothed wife to his companion, Samson caught three hundred foxes, tied them in pairs, lit a torch between their tails and let them loose through the fields. This may sound like an anger management issue, but do not neglect the fact that foxes can run between thirty to forty miles per hour. So, never mind that it is practically impossible for any human being to catch just one fox, but what about catching three hundred of them? You see, my friend, in specific seasons, or in specific situations, God will give you unlikely favor or ability to do what may seem impossible to man, because you are unique and you are a very significant individual.

Do not exchange your God-given identity or your kingdom purpose for a one-night stand with the devil.

Sleeping with Your Enemy

When Samson decided to play games with Delilah, he eventually "shot himself in the head" as though it were a game of Russian roulette. When you play with fire, you will get burned. When you entertain a venomous snake, then it is a matter of time until it bites you. And whenever you flirt with sin, sooner or later you will pay the price for it. The enemy of our soul is continually walking around like a hungry lion seeking whom he may devour.

Delilah accused Samson with these powerful and deceptive words, "How can you say, 'I you love,' when your heart is not with me?"[3] Whenever you begin to bond a relationship with the enemy of your identity, then it is just a matter of time until you become blinded to the great purpose that God has predestined for you. Just like Samson was literally blinded when his eyes were put out by his enemies, the Philistines.

Tragically, many Believers had their identity and purpose plucked from them by the enemy of their soul. And these same Believers continue to live their lives, attend church, read the Bible, and even pray, but they do not realize that their vision lays dormant in their spirit man. When you choose to sleep with your enemy or even flirt with him, then do not become surprised if that serpent of old robs you of your kingdom identity and purpose.

Sleeping with your enemy is also a sign of your unfaithfulness to God, even though He will always remain faithful to you. And the tragic story of Samson is once again a sobering reminder that the enemy to your God-given identity and purpose will utilize whatever tactics necessary in order to delay or to divert you from fulfilling your assignment on this earth. Additionally, Samson knew very well that it was Delilah that attempted to reveal the source of his strength by binding him with the fresh bow strings, then with the new ropes, and then by weaving his hair into the web of the loom. But he still chose to ignore all of the warning signs. In like manner, God will graciously give us plenty of warning signs, but the choice will always be up to you and I whether we will continue to flirt with the enemy of our soul.

Your purpose and calling does not exempt you from the consequences of your foolish or selfish choices.

Have You Seen My Wig?

If Samson would have put on a wig, would that have restored his strength? Sometimes we fool ourselves by thinking that our selfish or wrongful choices could be quickly and easily fixed. The Scripture records that it took some time for Samson's hair to grow back and still he had to pray to God to restore his strength so he could, for the final time, glorify God by killing many Philistines.

Yes, the grace and the mercy of our God is without measure, but we should not fool ourselves into thinking that when we willfully chose to get out of the will of God, we can just as quickly be restored. Sometimes our restoration is instantaneous, but other times it could take a while. Yes, Samson did glorify God in his final moment of life, but I doubt that this was God's perfect will for Samson to have been blinded and then to basically commit suicide as he broke the pillars that held the temple together as he killed the Philistines as well.

God's will is divine and perfect, but our wrongful choices are destructive and carry many unpleasant consequences. It is not God's will for you to have a child out of wedlock, or to be in a wheelchair because of your drunk-driving accident, or to go through a divorce, or to even die prematurely. I have heard plenty of preachers who would say that God uses sickness or other unpleasant circumstances to keep us humble, which has absolutely no biblical sustenance.

With that said, it was not in God's original plan for Samson to have his eyes put out or to die as a blind biblical hero. In similar manner, it gives no joy to our heavenly Father to see His children making foolish, reckless, and even deadly choices, which carry a ricochet affect throughout the rest of their lives. But, can God still powerfully use you in the near future when you have had a child out of wedlock? Absolutely yes! But it will not be in a way that was originally intended, since your child has now become one of your key priorities in your life.

Many try to play the game of ignorance by trying to justify their sinful lifestyle or consequential life choices by thinking that all will still be well once they give their life to the Lord or sincerely repent. Yes, I believe in divine forgiveness and restoration, but God cannot restore the lost years, or put your child born out of wedlock back into your womb, or grow back your missing limb that you lost due to stupidity, or any other severe health issues that you brought upon yourself. Sure, Jesus, through the power of the Holy Spirit and by His blood can heal any disease and sickness or miraculously grow back any missing limb, but oftentimes, that is not the case.

This may seem a little harsh on my part, but throughout the Bible and throughout history we have more than enough evidence to speak boldly on this subject matter. Time and time again we face the truth that God's will is perfect and divine, but it is our wrongful and foolish choices that derail us from His perfect will for our life, just like it did for Samson. But as I conclude this chapter, one thing we can always count on is God's endless grace, mercy, and forgiveness which was also evident in the final hours of Samson's life.

God's perfect will is for us to grow in our purpose and calling, and to remain in it just like Samson's hair grew and never saw the razor before his disobedience. Remember, Satan would love to craftily deceive you into exchanging your God-given identity for his fake wig. But the identity of Samson is a great reminder for us not to fall for that age-old trick. Again, Samson will remain one of the most talked about biblical characters from whom we can take away numerous practical life lessons to help us to stay faithful to our Lord Jesus and not allow the enemy of our soul to blind us to our kingdom calling.

When you discover and begin to understand the significance of your identity and purpose, only then you will begin to set specific boundary lines and disciplinary actions in your life.

Takeaway Lessons from the Life of Samson

- You and I should never be fearful or intimidated by how high or how far God can take us, since it is the gift within us that will make room for us.
- Your uniqueness is a sign and a confirmation that God has a specific calling and purpose for you.
- Repentance and humility before the Lord are key components to breakthroughs, restoration, and walking and living in victory.

18
THE IDENTITY OF NAOMI AND RUTH
The Power and Purpose of Mentorship

The lovable story of Naomi and Ruth resonates on how valuable the relationships in any family should be. Ruth was an outsider and she told her mother-in-law Naomi that she would make Naomi's *God her God and Naomi's people her own people.* In other words, when you discover your God-given identity and purpose, you will be willing to get out of your comfort zone, to geographically relocate, to go into unfamiliar territories, and to connect with people whom you may not know.

Ruth, at first felt like an outsider in the midst of Naomi's culture and people, but God had a greater plan for her life. In similar manner, because of God's calling upon your life, He will give you much favor amongst people whom you do not know and in areas you are not familiar with, like Boaz extended his favor towards Ruth and told his servants to leave behind crops in the field for her to gather. God in a similar way will give you much favor and will direct people into your life who will provide all of the necessary things that will help you fulfill your kingdom assignment on this earth.

With that said, we should not ignore the important role that Naomi, Ruth's mother-in-law, fulfilled in the life of Ruth. God used her to help Ruth discover her identity and purpose. Even though Naomi went through unpleasant tragedies in her own life by losing her husband and her two sons, she still submitted to God's purpose and will and God used her as a powerful life coach and a mentor in the life of her daughter-in-law, Ruth. And in this chapter, you will discover that no trials or hardships of life can ever stop you from fulfilling your kingdom assignment. I will also cover the importance of mentorship and the role of spiritual fathers and mothers, and finally, we will discover that your destiny is awaiting you at the feet of Christ.

Fierce opposition, harsh criticism, or fiery trials should only be seen as tools that are finetuning your identity and kingdom purpose.

Fiery Trials of Life Should Keep You More Focused on Your Purpose

Naomi's life was not easy but full of fiery trials when she lost her husband and then she lost both of her sons. When she decided to go back to her own people, she said these words to her two daughter in-laws, "No, my daughters; for it grieves me very much for your sakes that the hand of the Lord has gone out against me!"[1]

Fiery trials or tragedies of life come to many unexpectedly, but this does not mean that all hope is lost. But one tragic outcome that arises from these unpleasant circumstances of life is that many Believers become discouraged and even bitter at God. Just like Naomi said, "The Lord has gone out against me,"[2] this tends to be the position of those who likewise are enduring heavy trials in their life. As long as we allow the devil to take our focus off of the sovereignty of God for our lives, we will begin to raise our fist against Him who is the author and the finisher of our life.

When Naomi came back to her people, she did not want them to call her Naomi, she asked them to call here Mara, which means *bitter*. You see, Naomi allowed her overwhelming family situation to make her heart bitter. So, she chose to cast aside her original name which means *pleasantness* and instead put on *bitterness*.

Again, many Believers daily face tragic or devastating circumstances that are eating away at their faith and at their trust in God. Usually it is in these dire situations where the enemy of our soul creeps in to divert us from our God-give purpose. And it is because when we are the most vulnerable is when the enemy attacks the strongest! Also, it is when we are the weakest that the enemy tries to devour our faith and our trust in our heavenly Father. Remember, your fiery trials of life should keep you more focused on your purpose, not running away from it!

Your purpose will become your inner drive that will allow you to go through various trials of life.

Bitterness Turned into Mentorship

As much as Naomi's life was full of fiery tries and a decision to call herself *bitter* instead of *pleasantness*, she eventually realized that she could play a very essential role in the life of Ruth. When Naomi learned that Ruth obtained favor in the eyes of Boaz, she began to mentor her and to give her sound advice, which eventually resulted in Ruth getting married to Boaz.

It is truly remarkable how Naomi turned her bitterness into mentorship. This is a very valuable lesson that we need to comprehend as we can take our most bitter seasons of life and turn them into testimonies or tools to assist, encourage, or offer hope to those who are struggling or going through a tough season.

Here is another powerful truth to take away, that whenever we touch any object, we leave behind our personal fingerprints, and if an investigation was to take place, then all that needs to be done is for the investigator to use dusting or ultraviolet ray light and they will be able to find our fingerprints on whatever we have touched. So, in like manner, our kingdom identity and purpose is like an invisible fingerprint that will be left upon the individual's life that we interact with and whatever we do in our kingdom calling. And likewise with our involvement in your family, at your workplace or business, in your community, or in your local church. This is why you have most likely heard someone say, "When this person came into my life, everything began to change." Or, "Because this person gave me money or helped me out, I was able to get back on my feet again." In other words, every day we are touching people's lives, whether we know it or not. And this is why mentorship is so essential.

So, mentorship become Naomi's new purpose in her latter days, and I believe that many seasoned Believers who are older can be powerfully used by God as spiritual fathers, mothers, role models or mentors in the life of a youth or a young adult. My heart has been always ablaze with passion for mentorship, especially mentoring the younger generation which is desperately in need of credible and genuine Godly role models and spiritual fathers and mothers.

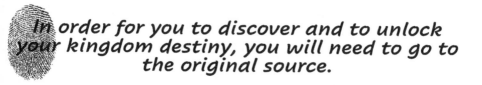

In order for you to discover and to unlock your kingdom destiny, you will need to go to the original source.

Your Destiny Awaits You at the Feet of Christ

The Bible is full of mysteries and some strange passages and in this case, we observe Ruth doing something very peculiar, per Naomi's advice. She came to Boaz, who was sleeping, and she uncovered his feet and lay next to them. As strange as this may sound, the final outcome of this bizarre deed led to her breakthrough and to her marrying Boaz.

This phenomenon implicates that when we humbly come to the feet of Christ, it is there where our destiny awaits us. To further note, around midnight, Boaz had a conversation with Ruth and told her to stay with him and she eventually laid at his feet until morning. Again, this further illustrates that Christ wants to commune with us all and for us to learn how to remain in His presence.

After Ruth was married to Boaz, she bore a son and called him Obed. Obed was the father of Jesse, who was the father of David. It is amazing that when we understand our purpose, we eventually discover our destiny, which has generational implications. How could Ruth have even imagined the fact that through her would arise a David, one of the greatest kings of Israel and part of the genealogy of Jesus?

The destiny of Naomi and Ruth exemplifies great partnership in the area of a mentor and mentee. This powerful duo speaks loud and clear to the importance that the body of Christ must have spiritual fathers and mothers and without them, the local and the global church will suffer a great setback.

Fulfilling your kingdom purpose will require the guidance and the wisdom of a mentor, and in due season you will also become a mentor to a mentee.

Takeaway Lessons from the Life of Naomi and Ruth

- Fiery trials, various tribulations, or unpleasant circumstances should only be looked upon as constructive instruments in your life.
- Never limit or restrict yourself from becoming an influential mentor, a life coach, or a role model in the life of another individual.
- Just like the disciples often sat at the feet of Christ, likewise you and I need to abide in His presence.

19
THE IDENTITY OF HANNAH
You Are Rare and Special

The first book of Samuel starts off with an intriguing story of a woman called Hannah. Now let us observe something interesting! This book in the Bible is titled as First Samuel, not as the book of Hannah! Again, when God really wants to get His point across, He will interject these interesting scenarios for all of us to seriously ponder on.

The first book of Samuel has a total of thirty-one chapters, but Hannah's story is only mentioned in the first two chapters. Again, this is something that we as God's children need to pay close attention to. Hannah did something out of the ordinary with her young son. She fully dedicated the baby Samuel to the Lord's temple to do the Lord's work. But this is only the beginning of this remarkable story, since we learn further on that Samuel heard the audible voice of God and was also raised in an unhealthy spiritual atmosphere with corrupt priests. And it is also fascinating that the Hebrew meaning of the name Hannah means *favor.*

As we follow the desperation of Hannah, the mother of Samuel, and her passionate heart, you will discover that, like Hannah, the gift embedded into your spiritual DNA is rare, special, and valuable. You will also learn that parents or parenthood is extremely imperative in any family structure. Because the parent becomes a tool in the hands of God as He uses the them to raise and direct their child towards their kingdom destiny.

Identity is like a rare stone. Once it is discovered, only then will you know its true value and worth.

You Are Rare and Special

Hannah understood that there was something special about her son Samuel, since she received him as a gift from God for an answered prayer. If only every parent could fully comprehend how valuable each and every single child that they bring into this world is, then they would have a whole different attitude and perspective on their role as a parent.

Hannah should become an encouraging role model for every parent, and especially for all mothers out there. The cry of Hannah's heart was to have a child, and the Lord honored her request, and in return, she fully dedicated her son Samuel unto the work of the Lord. Every parent should adhere to the spiritual lesson here, that there is power when we dedicate our children to the Lord for His greater purpose and will for their life. Also, I want to stress the point that single parents are not neglected by the Lord, but also have the exact same opportunity to dedicate their son or daughter for the greater kingdom purpose on this earth.

When you discover how rare your gift is, only then will the world have a great demand for you. The youthful Samuel carried the calling of a prophet whom the Lord used powerfully in the life of King Saul and King David. But it is a challenge for any parent to understand that their son or daughter carries within themselves a kingdom gift that has tremendous value and worth, and this gift needs to be first discovered and then released into the world. Whenever this occurs, your son or daughter will become a valuable asset and a magnificent tool in the hands of our heavenly Father.

The identity of Hannah is not strictly limited to a biblical character, but it can also apply to every parent on the face of this earth when they realize what a critical role they play as a parent in helping their son or daughter discover, understand, and release their God-given destiny, identity, and purpose.

As you fully trust the Lord, He will then be able to direct your kingdom assignment.

Takeaway Lessons from the Life of Hannah

- Your identity will let you know how rare you are.
- Your identity and purpose have been engraved into your spiritual DNA by God, which automatically makes you special and a valuable asset on earth.
- Prayer is a key component to fulfilling and operating in your kingdom assignment, but prayer (a type of faith) without works is dead.

20
THE IDENTITY OF SAMUEL
Your Destiny May Be Wrapped-Up in a Strange Package

The young Samuel is recorded as the youngest individual in the Bible who heard the audible voice of God. Most biblical scholars suggest that the young Samuel was between eight to twelve years old at the time. Samuel was also growing up and was mentored by the corrupt and spiritually tainted priest Eli who has not heard the voice of the Lord in long time. Not only that, the priest Eli had two sons who served in the temple but lived in sexual immorality and indulged themselves in the meat offerings.

Is it possible to grow up around immoral individuals and much corruption and still faithfully serve the Lord? Absolutely, yes! Is it possible to be surrounded with ungodly and corrupt individuals and still grow in your purpose and potential? Yes! And is it possible that God may use people in your life that seemed to be wrapped in strange packages? Yes!

Throughout this chapter I want to place most of the emphasis on the life of the young Samuel, before he became a great prophet of the Lord. Because his youthful upbringing plays a very essential part to why he became one of Israel's greatest prophets. And most importantly, the young Samuel speaks loudly to the fact that our excuses will never justify us from not living a life of holiness and purity.

Purpose is the discovery of the original reason for your birth and for your existence.

This Is Not Fair

This is not fair! Life is not fair! Why was I born like this? How come I do not have what others have? Yes, life is not fair and is full of injustice, setbacks, betrayal, and backstabbing. And if anyone had the right to complain then it would be the young Samuel. He was given away by his mother for adoption. He grew up and was raised in an unhealthy spiritual environment. But thus far, he is recorded as the youngest individual in the Bible to have heard the audible voice of God.

77

More and more, our culture grooms individuals to be selfish and self-centered and the younger generation is the primary target. But I am grateful that we have a remarkable role model in the Bible by the name of Samuel, who exemplified that no matter how unfair life may be, as long as we keep our heart and our focus on the Lord, He will give you the needed strength, power, and victory to overcome any and all temptations of life.

Your excuses will never exempt you from walking in your destiny or fulfilling your purpose.

You Have No Excuses

Regardless of how unfair Samuels early childhood and upbringing was, he still submitted to his unrighteous spiritual leaders and eventually became one of the greatest prophets of Israel. Another thing that Samuel did is not choose to sing the "my excuses" song, the top billboard song in the body of Christ. Rather, he chose to have no excuses in his mindset.

Those who take shelter behind their own excuses are advocating their hopelessness before others. They also use excuses as a substitute for not fulfilling their kingdom assignment. And I have already pointed out in previous chapters that the excuses of Moses and Gideon fell short of the ears of the Lord, and so will yours.

The lessons learned from the identity of Samuel should nullify every excuse in your mind as too many Believers have already aborted their kingdom assignment on earth. Because of this problem, the local church is in a deficit, and the body of Christ is spiritually limping. One of the reasons for this may be that your destiny is wrapped up in a strange package and because of this, many miss out or get discouraged in the process of the discovery and the understanding of their kingdom purpose on this earth. But the story of Samuel should encourage you and set your mindset into the right spiritual alignment as you allow the Lord to do what He is an expert at doing.

We may not have a choice of what type of purpose and assignment we will receive from the Lord, but we do have the privilege and the honor of discovering them.

Hearing the Voice of the Lord

Hearing the voice of the Lord is not some kind of an exaggerated religious notion that we talk about in our Christian faith. Hearing the voice of the Lord is an everyday essential duty for every born-again child of God. If I could take it a step further, I would honestly have to say that hearing the voice of the Lord falls into the top three issues or struggles that most, if not all Christians struggle with or have struggled with in their early years.

Hearing the voice of the Lord is not meant to be a cute suggestion or a savory sound pitch coming from the pulpit, but something that every born-again individual understands and practices in their daily walk with the Lord. I guess the challenging question that most encounter like I did in my early walk with the Lord is, "What does God's voice sound like?" Or, "How can I hear the voice of the Lord?" Or, "Does God still speak to His children like He did in the Bible?" All of the above questions are real and one of the greatest answers that I have ever heard was, "God's voice sounds exactly like your voice." Wow! That statement cast aside all of my confusion about what it means to hear the voice of God.

The important lesson here is that God did not limit His voice or His conversations to the prophets of the Bible or to the biblical leaders whom we admire. Hearing the voice of the Lord is essential and mandatory for every born-again child of God. So, if you desire to discover or to understand and to function in your kingdom assignment and purpose on this earth, you must be hearing the voice of the Lord in your spirit man. It will help and guide you in discovering who you are in Christ and who you are through Christ, as you fulfill your kingdom purpose.

The more you know the voice of the Lord the less doubt you will have about your calling and purpose.

Takeaway Lessons from the Life of Samuel

- The more quality time you spend with God, the clearer you will be able to hear His voice.
- We are all born into a corrupt world and that is why this world needs you and your kingdom gifts to be manifested.
- Immoral culture, sexual perversion, or temptations should never be a justifiable excuse as to why you are not able to fulfill your kingdom assignment on this earth.

21

THE IDENTITY OF KING SAUL

Your Life Contains Existential Value and Worth

King Saul obtained an honor and a privilege when he becoming Israel's first king, but he also became a disgrace in the eyes of God! Numerous teachings and sermons have been given because of Saul's, jealousy, power hunger, disobedience to God, and the list just goes on.

King Saul seemed to have some credible excuses before the prophet Samuel. When he disobeyed the commandment of the Lord and Samuel rebuked him, King Saul's reply was, "Because I feared the people and obeyed their voice."[1] This was one of the first signs of Saul's identity crisis. As a king, you do not heed the screaming or the complaining voices of your people or the overriding human opinions replacing the Word of the Lord! But that is exactly what he did.

When King Saul realized that he sinned before the Lord, his reply to Samuel is surprising: "I have sinned; *yet* honor me now, please, before the elders of my people and before Israel, and return with me, that I may worship the Lord your God."[2] Let us break that one verse down piece by piece since this one sentence is so profound that you could write a sermon series out of it:

- *I have sinned; yet honor, me now*: No remorse or conviction for sinning and Saul was also very proudful.
- *Please*: Saul was in great desperation, but it was a desperation for honor, and not for repentance.
- *Before the elders of my people and before Israel:* Saul did not want to lose his reputation before his subjects or in his kingdom domain.
- *Return with me that I may worship the Lord your God:* Saul just exposed that he had no personal relationship with the One who has chosen him to be king by saying, *your God*, not *my* God!

Every believer, especially pastors and church leaders, needs to seriously grasp the insight of this one verse, because it clearly shows that King Saul had no relationship with God and was more concerned about his reputation and status before man, instead of having the fear of the Lord and reverence for his Creator. And one of the easiest ways to see if someone has a serious spiritual identity crisis is when they have lost their personal relationship with God and have become more focused on the things of this world instead of the things of God.

In this specific chapter, I want to take a totally different approach by addressing a serious issue in our current culture that is spreading like a virus throughout the world, and that is a virus called suicide. And King Saul is a great example to this modern-day phenomenon.

Knowing your identity and purpose will make you deaf to people's opinions about you.

A Worldwide Virus Called *Suicide*

Many sermons and leadership lessons have been taken from the life and the deeds of King Saul, but very little emphasis is placed on the fact that Israel's first appointed king committed suicide. In chapter thirty-one of First Samuel we read, "Therefore Saul took a sword and fell on it."[3] I guess the crucial question that we all need to ask is, "How does someone like Saul who was anointed as Israel's first king go from such a glorious status to committing suicide?"

This unthinkable tragedy does provide great insight on how someone could be the most powerful, the most influential, the most successful, or the most admirable person, but because they are inwardly lost, confused, depressed, and lack the understanding of who they are in Christ, a lot of times these individuals lives tragically end in suicide. Just in recent years we have witnessed individuals of great success, popularity, or status who prematurely ended their lives:

- *Robin Williams*: One of Hollywood's greatest comedians who brought much laughter through his movie roles but ended up committing suicide at the age of 63.
- *Kate Spade*: A famous fashion designer committed suicide at the age of 55. She also reportedly left a suicide note to her 13-year-old daughter.
- *Anthony Bourdain*: Was a celebrity chef, author, and a famous travel documentarian who killed himself by hanging at the age of 61.

- *Tyler Honeycutt*: Played for the NBA team Kings, and after many hours long standoff with officers, he killed himself at the age of 27.
- *Matthew Warren*: The son of a Rick Warren, a well-known pastor and author, who took his life at the age of 27.

How is it that someone like Robin Williams could bring joy and laughter to the hearts and souls of millions around the world, but he himself inwardly struggle with severe depression?[4] How could someone like Kate Spade who added much beauty and prestige to the fashion design industry and causing millions to wear her brands and feel special, but Kate herself could not discover her inner God-given beauty and purpose on this earth? And how could someone like Anthony Bourdain who captivated the taste buds of people around the world through his passion for food, somehow not fully discover the inner passion for life on this earth?

The deaths of all the above individuals are extremely tragic, and we all need to take the matter of suicide seriously. Suicide is a tough and a sensitive issue that is sweeping around the world like an unstoppable virus. We should not take this issue lightly, but as Believers, we should not forget that He came to set the captives free and no darkness can resist the power of the Holy Spirit and the blood of Jesus that can deliver anyone from the thoughts of suicide.

I also want to shed some more light on this dark issue. To my surprise, I have also heard from the Christian community, including some prominent leaders, that suicide is a mental health issue. Sure, that is true in some cases! But hearing so much emphasis placed by born-again Believers that this is primarily a mental health issue is actually an issue in itself, since we cannot neglect that this is also a spiritually demonic issue. Let us not forget that King Saul was often troubled by a distressing spirit.[5]

Please do not misunderstand my heart here, I am in support of utilizing medication, counseling, and other medical treatments while we as Believers also pray and use all of the available options to help those who are struggling with suicide. But we also cannot be ignorant to the fact that no one with a sound mind just makes a decision to end their life unless there are demonic forces at play that are tormenting and terrorizing that heart and the mind of that particular individual. This also occurred with Judas Iscariot.

The more I follow the patterns of those who commit suicide, the more I come to the understanding that most of these precious individuals have come to a dead-end road in their life, thinking that there is no other hope for a brighter future that awaits them, and as a result they take their life into their own hands. But when I read about the Author and Finisher of our faith, He declares, "'For I know the plans *and* thoughts that I have for you,' says the Lord, 'plans for peace *and* well-being and not for disaster, to give you a future and a hope.'"[6]

And I pray for everyone who is reading this and is battling with thoughts of suicide to always know that your Creator, who is also your heavenly Father, loves you and has created you on purpose and for a purpose.

King Saul was full of glory, glamour, and influence and also full of darkness and tragedy. But this is not how God originally intended Saul's life to be. With that said, God is a giver of life while Satan is the executioner. We need to continually guard our hearts and our minds as we tune our ears to the giver of life and tune out the demonic voices that speak loudly in contradiction to the Word of God.

Knowing your identity and purpose will give you inner convictions, but the absence of them will make you vulnerable to plenty of addictions.

Takeaway Lessons from the Life of King Saul

- It is your personal relationship with the Lord that gives you your credibility and influence before others, and not your title, popularity, or good looks.
- Those who are facing a spiritual identity crisis become a direct target for Satan.
- Knowing your identity in Christ and your identity through Christ will give you the meaning for why you live and for what purpose you are living.

22
THE IDENTITY OF DAVID
Facing Your Giants

I purposefully chose to title this chapter as "The Identity of David" and not as "The Identity of King David"! Before David became one of Israel's greatest king's and most talked about biblical heroes, he was first a rugged looking teenager who just seemed like an ordinary kid. But it was in his younger years that we witness and discover the importance of his God-given identity.

I want to take the opportunity to primarily focus on the younger years of David, since they played a crucial role in his discovery and understanding of his identity and kingdom destiny. In this chapter, I will focus on how you can go from being an ordinary individual to becoming extraordinary. Also, I will cover the importance of knowing that you cannot carry or walk in someone else's identity, and finally, you will understand why your identity will go through different phases and trials.

The day you discover your purpose and identity will become the day when you will discover which giants you need to slay and overcome.

Going from Ordinary to Extraordinary

Who would have thought that this teenage shepherd boy would one day become a giant killer and a future king over Israel? Definitely not David's father Jesse! When the prophet Samuel came to Jesse's house and broke the news to him that God was choosing one of his sons to become the next king, Jesse then presented all of his sons before the prophet, with the exception of the teenager David. After God rejected all of Jesse's sons, the prophet posed an interesting question: "Are all the young men here?"[1]

Jesse's lack of insight or lack of belief is nothing new. Many parents do not always understand God's plan for their son or daughter. Some parents may even become in direct opposition to the will of God for their child's life since what their child is desiring to pursue does not make any sense to the parent or seems to be crazy. Just like Jesse made an ignorant mistake with David, his youngest son, I would like to challenge and even encourage every parent who will reads this to trust God with your heart and not with your head in regards to your son's or daughter's purpose and identity.

No parent is gifted with special foresight of whom their child will be or become in the near future. But God does provide, with time, small bits and pieces that we as parents need to put together as we move forward with our child or children through their growth and development process. And it is in this process that we begin to discover that our child is being changed from an ordinary teenager to an extraordinary vessel in the hands of the Almighty God.

Your past, your present, and your future are your classrooms where you learn; where you grow; and where you eventually take your final kingdom assignment exams.

Watch for Unusual Patterns and for Unusual Events

If I may, I would like to take a quick theological risk here! I do not believe that David's brothers, or his parents, ever knew that this teenager killed a lion and a bear while he was shepherding the sheep. Perhaps the first discovery of this occurred when David stood before King Saul and told him how he bravely killed the lion and the bear and that he was not afraid to face the giant Goliath.

The point that I am trying to illustrate here is that most often, many individuals, especially from our own family may not know our personal lions and bears that we have been fighting with and because of much familiarity that occurs within the family circle, we usually do not focus our attention on what God is doing in the life of our sibling or in the life of our child. In other words, what you do in your private life while others are not looking will eventually come to light, whether it is good or bad. In addition, God usually uses these private moments to teach all of us how to slay these lion or bear-type of situation so He can develop and teach us to discover our hidden, God-given potential and purpose.

One of the biggest questions I used to ask myself and others in my early years and the same question many of you ask today, is, "How do I discover my identity, purpose, and calling from God?" This is a very important question and we should not be ignorant of it. One of the ways that has helped me, and which I have been also utilizing when I disciple or coach others, is to pay attention to specific patterns or unusual events that occur in life.

For example, what book genre's interest you the most? What type of movies or TV shows do you enjoy watching? What things do you usually talk about? What dreams and desires do you have? Do keep in mind that all of the above things will not one hundred percent accurately depict your purpose and calling, but they will definitely give you some great insight. Again, be on a lookout for certain patterns and unusual occurrences that take place throughout your life since these are clues that God is revealing to you.

People will judge and limit you in accordance to their restricted understanding of who you are, but God is the only One who truly knows who you are.

God Does Not See Like Man Sees

The prophet Samuel received a reality check from the Lord, which became a powerful revelation for him, and for all who read this, when the Lord said, "For the Lord does not see as man sees; for man looks at the outward appearance, but the Lord looks at the heart."[2] Often we have made, and still continue to make, grave mistakes as we begin to see others through our limited, carnal standpoint and neglect to see the heart and the calling of that particular individual.

Many pastors and church leaders have neglected or overlooked individuals who carried God's anointing and assignment for their local church, just because these leaders looked at the outward appearance of that person instead of their heart. This has actually occurred in my personal life, when I attended my first church, and for many years, the pastors and elders did not see the gift and the calling in my life. Parents, likewise, have made similar grave mistakes with their children. Similarly, David's brothers saw a sheep herder, but God saw a giant slayer and a king of Israel. Remember, God does not see like man sees and this in itself should be a very encouraging thought.

The growth and the maturity of your assignment and calling will take time and various seasons of preparation.

A Green Strawberry or a Mouthwatering Mango?

What would have happened if David just stormed onto the battlefield to fight Goliath? Yes, he would still have had the victory, but he would have also gotten himself into some issues with King Saul. What I am trying to say here is, just because you have discovered your identity and purpose does not give you radical freedom to do whatever you desire or whatever you want. If you are called to preach, you just do not invite yourself to a church or a conference and begin preaching. If you are called to politics, you do not just walk into your local government office and ask for a position or ask to be placed on the next election ballot.

In similar manner, David first had to go to King Saul to inform him that he was willing to fight the giant. Once King Saul understood who David was and how he killed a lion and a bear, only then did Saul gave him permission to go fight Goliath. This is also true for us all. If you believe that God has called you towards something specific, then you first need to do some homework by asking yourself these basic questions:

- Does my gift and purpose require a college degree or an advanced education?
- What books do I need to read or what conferences and seminars do I need to attend?
- Where can I find a mentor who will be able to teach me, to train me, to educate me, and to guide me through my development process?
- What specific individuals, groups, associations, or organizations do I need to connect or network with?

By answering the above questions, you then begin to place yourself into a healthy position for growth, and in due time, the Lord will begin to open specific doors of opportunity for your gift to be able to manifest itself. You see, no one will enjoy the taste of an unripe mango, but everyone's mouth will water from a ripe luscious mango. And in like manner, when your inner gift is spiritually ripe (or mature), then everyone around you will enjoy the fruits of your labor.

 **identity is only compatible to you and to you alone.**

King Saul's Armor

Never make the crucial mistake by trying to wear someone else's identity. After David had a great conversation with King Saul, the king clothed David with the full armor that he used in his own battles. But something powerful come out of the mouth of David when he said, "I cannot walk with these, for I have not tested *them*." And then David took off King Saul's armor.

You would be making a grave mistake by trying to wear someone else's armor (or their identity and purpose). I am sure when we were growing up, we used to say something like this: "When I grow up, I want to play basketball like Michael Jordan." Or, "I want to be as smart and as wealthy as Bill Gates." Or, "I want to be anointed and influential like Billy Graham." There is nothing wrong with having such desires, but to try to take on someone's God-given identity and become a duplicate version of that person does have catastrophic consequences.

In David's case, he knew that his potential consisted in a slingshot, which he had already tested on a lion and on a bear. But King Saul's armor, he had *not* tested. Every individual has something specific and unique that is solely ascribed to them by our heavenly Father, but trying to mimic, copy, or duplicate someone else's anointing, gifting, or kingdom assignment will only result in a devastating outcome.

 **Never limit or restrict your kingdom assignment to a specific season in your life.**

Your Identity Will Develop in Different Phases and Trials

Before David ultimately stepped into his full assignment as a king over Israel, he first fulfilled an important role as a military leader in Saul's army. And because of David's great success as a military leader, he became loved by many while despised by his king, who also became his father-in-law.

Because of Saul's jealousy and envy towards David, he desired to kill him. As a result, David had to flee, and for many years, he was on a continual run from the king, who was tirelessly determined to kill David. Just as much as David had gone through different phases and trials in his life, in like manner, we will also have various phases and seasons of transition, which will also usher in different types of trials that will continually test us.

Just as every born child goes through the phase of crawling, then sitting, then standing, then walking and eventually running, also the development of our inner identity and purpose must go through phases. This developmental process is never easy and only those who fully surrender to the Almighty hand of God will be the ones who will walk and function in the fullness of their kingdom purpose.

The life of David as a teenager and as a king is momentous, and whether you are young or old as you are reading this, the identity of David can definitely speak volumes into your life and into your identity development. Your identity development will go through different phases and trials for the sole purpose of maturing you and making you into a useful tool in the hands of God.

Your kingdom purpose will never be intimidated by giant-sized obstacles or manmade limitations.

Takeaway Lessons from the Life of David

- Knowing your kingdom identity will give you the boldness to face or confront your giants.
- The day you discover your identity and calling will be the day when your shepherd-like mindset will transition into kingdom thinking.
- Never despise or ignore your slingshot-like gift, since God will use it to strike down every giant-sized opposition or to obtain a giant-sized opportunity.

23
THE IDENTITY OF SHAMMAH, ELEAZAR, JOSHEB-BASSHEBETH, ABISHAI, AND BENAIAH

Be Whom God Has Created You to Be

K ing David was surrounded with great counselors, advisors, and remarkable warriors. The Bible identifies chief men who were among the men named as David's mighty men:

- *Shammah*: He positioned himself in a field to defend it and eventually killed every Philistine that came his way.
- *Eleazar*: He fought until his hand was weary and was actually stuck to the sword.
- *Josheb-Basshebeth*: Killed eight hundred men at one time.
- *Abishai*: Killed three hundred men with a spear.
- *Benaiah*: Killed well-known heroic enemy warriors and also killed a lion on a snowy day.

In this unique chapter, I will outline the importance of you being whom God has created you to be. And you will also take away powerful truths about God dispersing various gifts, talents, abilities, and skills to everyone. In this chapter I will also encourage you to keep you mind open to the fact that your mission and assignment on this earth could be in a variety of areas, such as the military, the law enforcement, the coast guard, or as a firefighter. Never limit God with what He has engraved into your spiritual DNA.

Our world already has too many duplicates who do not know their identity. Be original! Be unique! Be yourself!

Be Whom God Has Created You to Be

I was originally born in the former Soviet Union and my Christian upbringing was extremely conservative. I was taught by my parents that it was a sin for a believer to have a gun or to carry a weapon into war with the intentions of trying to kill someone. When I moved to America, this same ideology continued for a while until I became a youth pastor and noticed how some of the graduating High schoolers expressed much interest in joining the military. And some did!

By that time, I had already gained a renewed mindset of guns and the military and I always blessed those who made the brave choice to protect the sovereignty of our country and the sovereignty of other nations. With that said, our military needs more kingdom-minded born-again Believers whom God will be able to use to reach out to their fellow soldiers and to become a beacon of hope to those who are spiritually dying.

Some of you may have a different perspective, or even a negative one, on our invasion into Iraq and our presence in other Muslim countries, but this has opened up doors of unorthodox opportunity for the Gospel message to go into territories that would have never allowed Christians to preach or to have churches. There were a good amount of Bible believing soldiers that held a rifle in one hand, but who also had a Bible in their pocket. They carried both a physical weapon and a spiritual weapon.

The mighty military men that surrounded David exemplify to us that our kingdom potentials do not need to be over spiritualized with supernatural powers of healing, signs and wonders, and the casting out of demons. There are, and will always be, numerous individuals who will not operate in the supernatural gifts that Apostle Paul outlines in First Corinthians,[1] but this does not mean that these same individuals are not anointed or do not possess kingdom abilities to be influential and impactful on this earth. And these radical mighty men of valor that surrounded King David do much justice by showing us that they were willing to sacrifice their own lives in order to protect the king and to fight for what was right.

Today, we have law enforcement officers, military personnel, body guards, coast guards, fire fighters, paramedics, security guards, and others whose jobs may seem that they are not spiritual or ministry based, but that is where we have made a grave mistake. On the contrary, all of the above positions are spiritual and can be considered full-time ministry. The issue is that we as Christians have over spiritualized everything and have also limited ministry to the four walls of our local churches, or to street evangelism, or to missionary work in other countries.

The identity and the calling of these mighty men of valor should especially encourage those Believers who are not employed in the full-time ministry of their local church, but occupy positions in the sphere of academics, the military, the government, the marketplace, the media, and the arts and entertainment. God has distributed different gifts, ministries, and activities by the same Spirit, for the purpose and for the profit of all.[2]

Your unique purpose and calling on earth can only be truly defined by our Heavenly Father and no one else.

Takeaway Lessons from the Life of Shammah, Eleazar, Josheb-Basshebeth, Abishai, and Benaiah

- The day you discover your God-given identity will be the day when you stop comparing yourself with others.
- Your gift carries a powerful spiritual connotation, even though you cannot find an exact Bible verse to define it.
- Fight the good fight and be the kingdom warrior whom God has created you to be.

24
THE IDENTITY OF ABSALOM
Honor Your Father and Mother

It is interesting to note that Absalom's name means, *father of peace*. But somehow it was he who stirred up a rebellion against his father, King David, which resulted in a coup and the takeover of the throne. For those who have studied the significance of Hebrew names and why they were given and what their true meaning is, you will understand that naming your child in those ancient days is not the same as today. The Jewish people took serious consideration on what names they would give to their children, especially their sons and especially their first-born

I am sure King David seriously considered the name and its significance when he called one of his son's Absalom. So, the big question is, how does a *father of peace* (Absalom), became a father of chaos and destruction? This scenario could also be attributed to Judas Iscariot who walked with Jesus for more than three years, or even Peter who denounced Jesus three times.

Just like Absalom, many Christians go through various trials and hurtful seasons in their life, which result in bitterness, hatred, and much divisiveness within their own family. Absalom could not forgive his brother for the sinful act that he committed against his sister, so he killed him. Then after his father, David, allowed him to come back into his presence, Absalom did nothing on his part to reconcile with his father, but only grew more bitter by the day.

The identity crisis that Absalom had is no different from what we could go through today, but when we choose not to deal with our identity crisis, then we could also create some grim outcomes in our personal life. The book of Proverbs states, "A cheerful heart is good medicine, but a crushed spirit dries up the bones."[1] And as we analyze the life of Absalom in this chapter, you will discover the catastrophic consequences of unforgiveness and the importance of honoring your father and mother.

Those who genuinely desire to know their inner identity and to function in their kingdom purpose will have to learn how to do a lot of forgiving.

Unforgiveness Is a Cancer to Your Identity and Purpose

Unforgiveness is a self-made prison in which you are the prisoner, the guard, and the jailhouse. It is also where you have placed the shackles upon your own hands and feet, and it was you who locked yourself behind the steel bars. So, you become imprisoned through your own personal choice, not by the fault of someone else.

The disciples of Jesus thought that they were very wise when they responded to His question in reference to forgiveness. But the Lord threw an unexpected curveball at them when He responded, "I do not say to you, up to seven times, but up to seventy times seven."[2] I'm more than sure that His disciples were not expecting that type of reply. The principle here is not about numbers or multiplication, but with having to do with the attitude and the condition of our heart.

Absalom became a victim to his own doings. Likewise, millions upon millions of Christians around the world bind themselves with destructive chains and imprison themselves. For some, their imprisonment lasts a day, while for others, their imprisonment endures for the rest of their life. When we bind ourselves with unforgiveness, we tend to ignore that by doing so we are limiting, restricting, and even expelling our kingdom purpose and assignment on this earth. Absalom could have become the next king after the death of his father David, but that never came to fruition, because his bitterness consumed his life to his own grave.

If you genuinely desire to fulfill your purpose on this earth and to discover whom God made you to be, then be willing to forgive and to forget, no matter how tough or tearful it may be. Remember, unforgiveness is a cancer to your identity and purpose.

Chastising and correction from the Lord keeps you humble and on the right path towards your destiny.

Honor Your Father and Mother

The Ten Commandments are not meant to be ten suggestions. Honoring your father and your mother was not a cute suggestion from God, but a stern directive, which carries a blessing or drastic consequence. The story of Absalom is tragic and should be attentively analyzed.

Yes, Absalom was angry because his sister was raped and dishonored by his fellow sibling, which resulted in him killing his own blood brother. To make things even worse, he conspired against his father King David, which resulted in a coup. Not only that, but he publicly shamed all of his fathers concubines as he had sexual relations with them in a tent on top of the king's house.

These horrific acts of dishonor, rage, and immorality against his family reflects much on what we are continually witnessing in our modern-day society and even amongst our fellow Believers. The lesson here is that when we cast aside God's Word or His commandments, we then begin to live a life that leads into a spiral downfall.

Unaccountable youth and teenagers have not grown to their adulthood and have never had their own families, just because they are buried in the cemeteries due to the fact of their disobedience to their parents. Many chose to despise, dishonor, or verbally and even physically abuse their parent, and because of certain acts of disobedience it has resulted in catastrophic or deadly outcomes, like drunk driving accidents, overdoses, suicide, rape, or even murder.

The New Living Translation boldly states, "Honor your father and mother. Then you will live a long, full life in the land the Lord your God is giving you."[3] The emphasis is placed on living a *long* and a *full life*. Honoring your parents is definitely a choice that each person needs to make for them self, but if that honor is absent, God cannot be unfaithful to His own Word and as a result, you will deprive yourself of your kingdom purpose or even shorten your lifespan on this earth.

The tragic outcome in the life of Absalom should never be justifiable because of the rape of his sister, and we also should neither convince ourselves that what happened to us or around us should become a reason for why we are bitter, angry, frustrated, broken-hearted, or depressed. These types of lame excuses will rob you of your joy, your happiness, your breakthrough, your prosperity, your health, and eventually your God-given identity. Exercise forgiveness and honor your parents and everyone around you. And then just watch what God is able to do in you and through you.

Do not shorten your life or get fired from fulfilling your purpose on this earth, just because you lacked the honor for your father or your mother.

Takeaway Lessons from the Life of Absalom

- Dishonoring your father or mother will place your kingdom assignment in severe jeopardy.
- Unforgiveness has the power and the authority to bind or to restrict you from reaching your destiny.
- As you dishonor or despise others, in like manner, others will dishonor or despise the gift that is within you.

25

THE IDENTITY OF KING SOLOMON

Knowledge Is Not Everything

Solomon—what divine wisdom he possessed! But is there a difference between just having everyday knowledge and having the wisdom that comes from God? Yes, there is a big difference, but I do want to also be careful, so it won't seem as though I'm against individuals obtaining knowledge or understanding in things that are needed for our everyday life or for our career purposes.

The Bible defines the wisdom that comes from God as the *Fear of the Lord.* Interesting! So, how does the fear of the Lord convert into wisdom? Again, the book of Proverbs exemplifies the fear of the Lord as:

- The beginning of knowledge[1]
- The beginning of wisdom[2]
- Provides strong confidence[3]
- The fountain of life[4]
- The instruction of wisdom[5]
- Departing from evil[6]
- Leads to life[7]

I guess the source for obtaining and operating in the wisdom of God lays in the fear of the Lord! Also, the three books that Solomon authored in the Bible speak for themselves. Proverbs, Ecclesiastes, and the Song of Solomon are so universal in their language and content that any person from any background, culture, or religious belief that read King Solomon's three books will receive much wisdom and knowledge. Proverbs and Ecclesiastes can be taught at leadership conferences and seminars or at business meetings. The Song of Solomon can be utilized in romance novels, in movies, or on Valentine cards.

I guess some of the troublesome questions we can consider are: How could a person of such wisdom have seven hundred wives and three hundred concubines? Or how could he, at the end of his days, begin to stray away from God and begin to erect idols of worship for some of his wives? This again underlines that we as human beings are full of weaknesses, but that should never be an excuse but only a reason on why we need to continually abide in the fear of the Lord. And the life of King Solomon has much wisdom to offer us as it pertains to our identity and our kingdom assignment on this earth, as you will learn in this chapter.

The fear of the Lord is the fuel to your kingdom assignment and calling.

How Much Is Too Much?

The wisdom that King Solomon possessed was remarkable. His wealth in today's currency is roughly estimated at around $500 billion. He built a temple for the Lord which was made out of gold and precious stones and was also considered as one of the wonders of the world. But in all of this wealth and wisdom, somehow he saw fit to have seven hundred wives and three hundred concubines (or girlfriends).

There is much wisdom and knowledge that we can draw from the Book of Proverbs and Ecclesiastes, which happen to be some of my favorite books in the Bible, but how can we blindly ignore the fact that Solomon technically had 1,000 female love companions and towards the end of his life began to build pagan idols?

When we study and evaluate all of these biblical personas, we have to analyze and understand the good, the bad, and the ugly side of each one. By doing so, we will not be ignorant to the fact that they were also human beings who had their own weaknesses and their own personal demons that they battled with. And in this case, King Solomon's greatest weakness was women.

The life and the identity of Solomon has much to offer to every believer, especially lessons about the dangers of having too much. And no, I am not limiting this to financial abundances only, which is often taken out of context within Christian teaching. Solomon was functioning in his purpose and calling, but also allowed his weakness to take control of him.

Here I want to point out that some of the dangers that we are all tempted with is that when God eventually raises us to the pinnacle of our success or wealth, that we do not allow all of the above to corrupt or to destroy us. Each and every person has their own weaknesses just like King Solomon had, and the devil will work in overtime mode in order to use that specific weakness against you, especially in your most vulnerable moments.

Having too much should not become a fancy religious slur that is used amongst Christians, but an opportunity to do a lot more for the kingdom of God. But getting out of your kingdom alignment by focusing more on material possessions or your achievements will sooner or later get ahold of you and will eventually divert you from your assignment. Stay focused, and continually ask God for more wisdom.

Keeping your heart in a healthy spiritual alignment will keep your head from getting too haughty.

Knowledge Puffs Up

Another valuable life lesson that we can take way from the wise King Solomon is that knowledge can puff up in our hearts faster than we think. First Corinthians states, "We know that we all have knowledge. Knowledge puffs up, but love edifies."[8]

Knowledge is great, but when too much knowledge overtakes your thinking, then you begin to ignore the prompting of the Holy Spirit. Our modern-day tech savvy generation with knowledge at the tip of their fingers, has been dumbing down many, especially amongst the younger generation. In other words, we have so many "highly educated" fools. They may be intellectual, but dumb as a doorknob when it comes to the issues of life.

God desires for us to be intellectual, smart, educated, and knowledgeable, especially as it pertains to your purpose and your kingdom assignment. But when you allow all of your head knowledge to get the best of you, then you begin to rely more on your intellect rather than on the guidance, wisdom, and the discernment of the Holy Spirit. The life of King Solomon offers us the insight that true wisdom and knowledge can only come from God and His Word. We need to be very careful not to put our trust into our educational degrees, human philosophies, or the deprived wisdom of this world.

The day you discover your identity and purpose will be the day when your destiny will become more viable.

Takeaway Lessons from the Life of King Solomon

- Allow your identity and purpose to function through your heart and not through your head.
- Learn how to be content with who you are, with what you have, and what God has entrusted you with until He gives you more.
- It is the fear of the Lord that will keep you on the right path towards your destiny.

26
THE IDENTITY OF ELIJAH
Your Victories Will Always Attract Your Enemies

T he life story of Elijah portrays a great example of how it is very likely that whenever you experience one of your greatest achievements, breakthroughs, or spiritual accomplishments that all of sudden, you feel that all of hell and its demonic agents have risen against you. This is exactly what occurred in the life of Elijah.

In this chapter, I will outline the importance of why we as God's children will face much opposition from the devil and from his demonic kingdom. As a believer, whether you want to believe in the devil and his demonic agents or not, still does not and will not exonerate you or exempt you from being resisted, especially if you are trying to fulfill the will of God in your personal life. Tragically enough, many of God's children have become victims to this powerful truth, just because they have foolishly ignored the fact that the devil is a vicious lion, always on a lookout for his next victim. And the life story of Elijah does draw forth powerful and insightful examples that those who choose to walk in their kingdom calling and to fulfill the will of God will become vulnerable to the attacks from the enemy of our soul.

How you respond or react to criticism, to opposition, to betrayal, or to various attacks will be determined by whether you know your inner identity or not.

Your Victories Will Always Attract Your Enemies

The prophet Elijah had a spiritual contest with the prophets of Baal to see whose God was real where he built the altar of the Lord and asked God to respond with a supernatural fire from heaven, and additionally, Elijah took these 450 prophets of Baal and executed them with his sword. I would have to say that this was a very successful and a powerful ministry event that went down in the history books, but this phenomenal event does not conclude here. Following this manifestation of God's glory and power, Elijah heard the news that Queen Jezebel wanted to kill him for what he just accomplished. Hearing this threat, Elijah put on his running shoes and fled into the wilderness and hid himself in a cave because of fear.

At our first evaluation, we can quickly become very judgmental of Elijah and his fearful response to Jezebel's threat. But before we cast our stone of criticism at him, let us first understand that often, after our greatest spiritual victory or breakthrough, will come some of the greatest attacks from the devil upon our life. Why? There are typically two primary reasons:

1. Your greatest victory, breakthrough, or accomplishment will attract the attention of the spiritual realm, and this usually results in a vicious attack from the enemy of your soul.
2. This is also a follow up evaluation that will allow you to test your heart and your motives, and learn how you and I need to place more trust on the grace of God like never before.

Many great men and women of God came crashing down after they had one of their greatest breakthroughs in their personal life, in ministry, or even in their business. And that is because the enemy of our soul is continually walking around "seeking whom he may devour"[1] and those who usually stand out the most will get his most undivided attention.

The identity of Elijah teaches us that doing the will of the Lord is a great blessing and a great privilege, but it is not always like eating a savory caramel candy. Doing the will of the Lord will always attract various attacks from the devil and much resistance from others. If you ignorantly think that you will be exempt from spiritual or demonic attacks, then you are either not reading your Bible correctly, or you are not functioning in your kingdom calling, or it could be that you have not done anything for the kingdom of God yet.

Another key factor to why your victories will attract your enemies, is because we live in a fallen world with individuals who have a fallen nature, unless they become born-again. And still, we have many in the body of Christ that are full of jealousy, envy, and covetousness towards their fellow brother or sister in the Lord. Always remember that those who stand out the most will become the most visible to the enemy of your soul. And victories or great breakthroughs will automatically make you stand out. When this occurs, this is a healthy sign of spiritual growth and maturity.

Knowing your kingdom purpose will give you a purposeful direction, a clear objective, an action plan, and a stronger vision.

Takeaway Lessons from the Life of Elijah

- If you do not want to experience any attacks or resistance from the enemy of your soul, simply do nothing for the kingdom of God.
- As sweet honey attracts the appetite of a vicious bear, likewise your breakthroughs, achievements, and victories will attract the devil, the vicious lion.
- Attacks or resistance from the enemy of your soul is a motivational encouragement that you are abiding in the will of God for your life.

27
THE IDENTITY OF JEZEBEL
The Spirit of This Age

The identity of Jezebel has much correlation with the identity of Lucifer, which I will share in more detail in chapter forty-five. Jezebel is an important historical figure who is often referenced as the "spirit of Jezebel" that is working against the body of Christ and especially against church leaders.[1]

The "Identity of Jezebel" is neither female nor male, but it is a spirit. And this spirit has a specific purpose and a specific agenda. Let us take a look at some of the most powerful tactics and weapons that this spirit utilizes against the children of God:

1. *Suicide*
2. *Rebellion*
3. *Fear and Depression*
4. *The Spirit of Religion*
5. *The Spirit of Feminism*
6. *Opposition to the Word of God*
7. *Abortion* (Both Natural and Spiritual)
8. *Division, Manipulation, and Witchcraft*
9. *Divorce* (the Destruction of the Family Unit)
10. *Sexual Immorality* (Adultery, Lust, Pornography, Gender Confusion)

Sadly enough, this spirit is both operating in the secular world and in the body of Christ. We see the identity of Jezebel's imprint in the social media, in Hollywood, in academia, in politics, in the marketplace, and in our culture. This should not surprise us at all, but the disturbing truth is how Jezebel's imprint is so evident amongst fellow Believers. In this chapter, I will outline the purpose and the agenda of the "Identity of Jezebel" and how it is successfully and tactfully moving through the body of Christ.

Your kingdom purpose and calling will often be tested through money, fame, and sex.

The Spirit of This Age

The Bible clearly records that Jezebel had most of the prophets under her control. This is similar to her having control and influence over pastors of our time. One of the most heartbreaking things to witness is how the "Identity of Jezebel" is alive and active in the body of Christ. Over my years as a believer and having been in church ministry for many years, I am still assured that those who operate under the influence of the "Identity of Jezebel" are those who have not discovered their God-given identity and purpose.

Now some of you could be stirred up with excitement thinking that I would be outlining a whole list of pastors, preachers, or ministers who supposedly operate under the "Identity of Jezebel." Sorry, that is not my cup of tea! My kingdom calling is not to be a spiritual police officer who is exposing false preachers or heretics in the body of Christ. But my desire is to point out the importance of how any of us could get lured into the things of this world, which include the lust of the flesh, the lust of the eyes, and the pride of life.[2]

The deceptive "Identity of Jezebel" cannot be only attributed to ministers or to church leadership, but to every born-again believer. Remember, Satan's fulltime job is to steal, to kill, and to eventually destroy. Whenever a believer chooses to position themselves to be neutral, politically correct, or none-offensive, then they do not notice that they are no longer standing out as a bright light of righteousness or holiness. They are no longer bringing kingdom influence into whatever atmosphere that they are in, but the opposite is true where the darkness is overshadowing their dimmed light and Jezebel's spirit is slowly luring this individual as a sheep into the slaughter house.

Why is the "Identity of Jezebel" also likened to "The Spirit of This Age"? Because she softly and gently speaks the things that you want to hear, the things which will not convict you, or the things that will not usher the fear of the Lord into your spirit man. And Timothy boldly stated, "But know this, that in the last days perilous times will come: For men will be lovers of themselves, lovers of money, boasters, proud, blasphemers, disobedient to parents, unthankful, unholy, unloving, unforgiving, slanderers, without self-control, brutal, despisers of good, traitors, headstrong, haughty, lovers of pleasure rather than lovers of God, having a form of godliness but denying its power. And from such people turn away!"[3]

The "Identity of Jezebel" also has another unique characteristic where it craftily masquerades itself behind manmade religion. And no, I am not referring to other world religions, but to so many religious doctrines and ideologies that have flooded into the body of Christ. Also, Jezebel has been increasing in an aggressive feministic spirit, that so many Believers, especially the younger generation, have been entrapped with. And Jezebel has been also stirring up many hearts with divisiveness, rebellion, and manipulations.

As much as this demonic identity carries so much power and is gaining so much momentum in today's culture and society, it is also banging hard on the doors of the body of Christ and screaming loudly against those who choose to live a life of holiness, righteous, and purity, those who are pro-life, and those who choose a lifestyle of morality. It is one thing that the world is spewing hatred against the children of God, but it is a whole different thing when those who call themselves Christians are also proud supporters of abortion, same sex marriage, the LGBTQ lifestyle, socialism, and have the attitude of "I can live however I want and do whatever I want."

The "Identity of Jezebel" continues to deceive the hearts of many in the body of Christ, and we need to use the Word of God and operate in the fear of the Lord in order to be able to discern what is the truth and what is a deception. And to also be able to stand for purity, righteousness, and holiness, as some may call these old religious ideologies. The "Identity of Jezebel" is a demonic spirit that could only take root in the hearts of those who do not know their identity *in* Christ or in those who have not discovered their identity *through* Christ, which is their purpose and kingdom assignment on this earth. Jezebel is the spirit of this age and only those who submit to the leading of the Holy Spirit will be able to discern or expose this demonic spirit.

Your specific identity and kingdom assignment will be strategically targeted and attacked by the enemy of your soul.

Takeaway Lessons from the Life of Jezebel

- If the truth of God's word offends you, then this is a sign of you being out of your spiritual alignment or you being out of the will of God.
- If you have not discovered your kingdom identity and purpose, then you become easily vulnerable to deception, to depression, to manipulation, and also being entangled into unbiblical ideologies or heresies.
- Those who are genuinely functioning in their kingdom calling will become aware and alert to the spirit of Jezebel and her demonic agenda.

28
THE IDENTITY OF ELISHA
Double for Your Trouble

W hen Elisha understood the prophetic gesture that Elijah gave him by throwing his mantle on him, Elisha slaughtered all of his oxen and offered them to his people. He burnt all of the equipment for the oxen, said farewell to his family members, and followed after Elijah. In other words, Elisha got rid of his business and left the marketplace sphere and went into the church ministry.

The identity of Elisha teaches us powerful principles on servanthood, faithfulness and what it means to endure until the end. When Elisha was called by the Lord through Elijah, he left everything and everyone behind and took on the mantle of his new kingdom assignment. This took boldness, obedience, and full commitment. And in this chapter, as we analyze the life of Elisha, we will understand why he asked for a double portion. It was not because of pride or self-ego, but because he understood something greater.

The discovery of your purpose and assignment will give you the boldness to make radical choices.

Double for Your Trouble

A few years ago, I had an interesting conversation with my wife where I backtracked all of the jobs I had and how I was treated while working at them. I reflected on how much I was underpaid, and how much advantage the management or the business owner took of me. After I outlined this in full detail to my wife, she was very surprised since she was not aware of these patterns and this eventually led to a very productive and interesting family conversation.

It felt that throughout my working career, I had been used as doormat that others would be wiping their dirty feet upon. This reality check was unpleasant and even disturbing. But through God's grace, I received in my spirit man this word, "Double for your trouble." And I began to understand that God will transform all of the trouble that I faced in my career path into blessings.

Many of us go through some long and strange seasons in our lives where we begin to question God and begin to doubt our purpose on this earth. This is nothing new, but the tragic outcomes often occur when many of God's children become too stressed out and eventually give up on their purpose and even give up on God. And in this particular story of Elisha, he had the opportunity to go back or to stay and not follow after Elijah as he was being taunted by others each time he went through a different town. But nevertheless, he held onto his heart's desire for a double portion and continued to follow Elijah until he was taken away by the fiery chariots.

One of the most powerful lessons that we can take from the life of Elisha is that, first, he was a faithful servant. And he was a faithful servant until the end. This qualified him to ask for, and eventually receive, a double portion of Elijah's spirit.[1] As a child of God, you would be making a dreadful error if you think that you can just simply inquire of the Lord for whatever your heart desires, but at the same time, not be willing to pay a price of servanthood or a price of faithfulness unto Him.

You see, your kingdom assignment on this earth requires anointing, favor, provisions, and the assistance and the networking of many, because by yourself you are not able to fulfill your kingdom assignment. Why? Because its bigger than you and no one is able to fulfill their kingdom assignment by themselves. And tragically, many Believers become spiritually exhausted and discouraged, because they expect much from God, but give very little of themselves to Him.

The principle of "Double for Your Trouble" is not limited to specific individuals. I have personally witnessed many Believers who have gone through some treacherous seasons of their life, and for those who remained faithful in whatever they were doing for the Lord, I now see how much they are blessed, and how much influence they have as kingdom ambassadors. I guess the challenge for us as God's children is to understand that we do not just easily walk into the fullness of our calling on this earth, but there is a price that we all need to pay. And do keep in mind that if you ever walk into a store and walk out with an unpaid item, then you will be considered a thief and will be arrested, unless you pay for that specific item. Our heavenly Father abides by the similar principles that He will not entrust His kingdom tools unto anyone, that is not willing to pay the price of righteousness, holiness, faithfulness, and full surrender to His will for your life.

Make a decision today, not to run after anointing or even after certain men or women of God, but to remain as a faithful servant and steward to the heavenly Father, and in due season, He will exalt you and He will release unto you your predestined portion.

__Your__ uniqueness will automatically qualify you for specific favor, fascinating connections, open opportunities, and for abundant rewards.

Takeaway Lessons from the Life of Elisha

- Your kingdom assignment has a specific reward.
- The day you discover and understand your kingdom purpose will be the moment when you will know your true value on this earth.
- Serving others is a personal choice and often your blessings are derived from your servanthood.

29
THE IDENTITY OF A YOUNG JEWISH GIRL
Nameless but Famous in the Bible

T he Bible is and will always be a very fascinating book. Why? The stories, the people, and the life applications that we read about are truly mesmerizing. And the story of the young Jewish girl speaks for itself. In this chapter, we will embark on discovering the boldness of a teenage girl who challenged her master, a commander in the Syrian army, to go to a prophet and be healed from his leprosy.

The fascination of this whole story does once again underline how awesome our God is. Let us observe some profound specifics:

- The young Jewish girl was taken into captivity.
- She was made into a house maid.
- She boldly challenged Naaman to go to a foreign land to get his healing.
- Naaman then went and told his Syrian king that a young captive girl told him that he could be healed.
- The king of Syria said, "Go now, and I will send a letter to the king of Israel."[1]
- Naaman traveled hundreds of miles towards Israel.
- Naaman stood at the Elisha's door, but the prophet never came out and only sent his messenger.
- Elisha's messenger tells Naaman to go to the Jordan river and wash himself seven times.
- Naaman becomes furious over this command, since the Jordan river was not as clean or pleasant as his rivers in Damascus.

The above outline once again demonstrates the uniqueness of this whole story that started because of a young Jewish girl whose name we will never know. And what else makes this story so special is that after Naaman received his healing, the Bible never again mentions anything in reference to this young Jewish girl. As you go through this remarkable chapter, you will discover that you do not need to be anyone special or anyone who possesses special talents or abilities, but you need only to entrust your life into the hands of the almighty God and just watch how He is able to powerfully use you for His kingdom purpose.

In God's original plan, He had you in mind personally when He created you, but it is up to you to discover this truth.

Who Said That Everyone Needs to Know Who You Are?

Who said that God does not have a sense of humor? Here is a young Jewish girl who is taken into captivity and then has the boldness to tell her captor what he needs to do in order to be healed. Surprisingly, Naaman who was a reputable commander in the Syrian army, heeded the suggestion of this young girl and went to see the prophet Elisha. Eventually he was fully healed and returned home with great joy. The interesting notion is that we never hear about the future fate or any other details of this young Jewish girl. For example: What was her name? Did Naaman free her from her captivity when he returned to his homeland? Did she receive riches and honor when he got back? All we know, was that she was a young Jewish girl who knew an almighty God of Israel.

The crucial question is, who said that everyone needs to know who you are? The truth is that you can never make yourself of any reputation or worth without the kingdom gift and the kingdom assignment that abides within you. It is your identity and purpose that will give you credibility, value, and worth before others. And if we can learn a powerful life lesson from the young Jewish girl, then it would be that she knew who she was and whom she served.

Your character and personality are a reflection of your inner kingdom identity.

Do Not Seek Fame or Recognition

This amazing story of how influential this young Jewish girl was is very unique, but the fact that this whole story is only expressed in just one chapter, is very intriguing. Can you imagine, that one of the most unique stories in the Bible is about a nameless individual and is also illustrated in one chapter? Here is a thought—could we live in such a way that our whole life could be summed up in just one chapter?

This young Jewish girl may have been nameless, but she did become famous as we are still reading her remarkable story thousands of years later. I guess the honest question we all need to ask ourselves is, do we need to be somebody extraordinary in order to have influence? No! Do we need to seek fame or recognition in order for our God-given purpose to become credible? Absolutely not!

Throughout my personal life I have come across a handful of individuals whom I thought were very genuine, credible, and have accomplished enough in their life in order to be highly spoken of or recognized before others. But to my surprise, they were just simple individuals who had a great heart and if I mentioned their names to others, then most folks would not know who they were.

Jesus, a handful of times, rebuked the religious leaders of His time on how they would seek after man's recognition or how they desired to be very reputable before others, but their hearts were evil and full of self-righteousness. Anyone who desires to seek fame or people's recognition will get it, but as soon as you fail them, then it will be these same individuals that will devour you.

When I say, "Do not seek fame or recognition," it is not meant to be a cute suggestion, but something that you and I need to take with serious consideration, since many have lost focus of pleasing and honoring the Lord and have become more occupied in pleasing others for the recognition honor. And as I conclude this remarkable chapter, do keep a healthy understanding and a humble heart knowing that you first walk before an almighty God and that it is He who gives you power, influence, and credibility before others, and it is also He who will open and close doors of opportunities. And it is also He who can take a nobody and make them into a somebody.

When you have discovered your kingdom destiny, you will no longer be intimidated or swayed by the thoughts and the opinions of others.

Takeaway Lessons from the Life of a Young Jewish Girl

- The more you understand your kingdom assignment, the less people's criticism or opinions of you will matter.
- Those who seek fame, recognition, or praises are individuals who are going through an identity crisis.
- You could live your whole life and be nameless before many, but there will always be those few who will always remember and cherish the deeds that you did for them or how you have impacted their life.

30
THE IDENTITY OF KING HEZEKIAH
Be Original and Standout from the Crowd

Y ou have probably heard this many times before that each and every human being has an original fingerprint. And it is this simple and profound truth that is one of the aspects that makes us unique and original. King Hezekiah understood this valuable principle, and that he might have been just another king over Israel, but he did not need to be like all other kings. He could be an original.

One of the key components to the life of King Hezekiah was him destroying the bronze serpent that Moses had built in the wilderness. The Israelites made this bronze image into an idol and worshiped it for many generations. Also, when the Assyrians besieged the city, King Hezekiah prayed and humbled himself before the Lord and the Lord sent one angel who killed one hundred and eighty-five thousand Assyrian soldiers in one night.

In this distinct chapter, you will discover the importance of being original and standing out from the rest of the crowd. Also, that your identity begins and ends with you. And finally, the importance of not following in the wrongful or the destructive steps of your father or mother who did not know or have not served the Lord. The life or the lifestyle of your ungodly parent does not need to become yours.

You may not have had a choice of having been born as a male or a female or a choice on who will be your immediate family members, but you do have a choice of what type of life you will live on this earth.

Your Identity Begins and Ends with You

Before Hezekiah became a king, his upbringing and background seems as though it was totally opposite of who he was and what he did during his reign as a king. Hezekiah's father, King Ahaz, did not do what was right in the sight of the Lord. Ahaz offered one of his sons as a human sacrifice, he burned incense in high places, and he took silver and gold out of the house of the Lord and gave it to the king of Assyria.

Hezekiah's father was considered one of the most evil and immoral kings that Israel ever had, but King Hezekiah turned out to be the opposite of his father. After Hezekiah destroyed and removed anything and everything that had to do with idol worship or idolatry, the Bible records King Hezekiah as one of the greatest righteous kings of Israel.

You see, your identity begins and ends with you! No one can take on your identity and you do not have to take on anyone else's identity either. Sure, parents do have a powerful influence and are role models to their child, but as the child grows older, they do not have to be the parent like they used to be, since their child has their our own personal will. I am sure that Hezekiah did not agree with his father's behaviors and immoral deeds, so he made a decision to worship the Lord and to restore the true identity of Israel during his reign.

We hear this so often: "It is not my fault that I grew up in a messed-up family," or "I never had a good father as a role model," or "My parent was abusive," or "My parent is in prison for breaking the law." Yes, your family environment and upbringing does develop you, but it does not have to define you! Have the heart attitude of King Hezekiah and make the right choices for your life and for your future.

Your identity acts as a spiritual magnet that will continually draw you to the original source, which is your Creator.

Know Your Original Source

When the Assyrian army besieged Jerusalem and mocked and threatened King Hezekiah, the king went into the house of the Lord to pray for deliverance and protection. Because of this, the Lord answered Hezekiah's prayers and He sent an angel who in one night killed 185,000 Assyrian soldiers.

No matter what challenges you will face, always know your original source. Hezekiah was a successful king, but Jerusalem and all of its citizens were in grave danger, so Hezekiah did not retreat or surrender before his enemy, but he retreated to the house of the Lord and surrendered himself into the hands of the Almighty God for his deliverance and breakthrough.

Remember, God created you as an original and it is your choice whether you want to blend in or stand out from the rest of the crowd. It is easy to do wrongful and evil deeds, but it will require much discipline and heart conviction to do what is right. It is normal for most of us to be self-centered, but it will require a selfless attitude if you desire to be people centered. King Hezekiah did not go on a campaign trail moaning, groaning, or complaining about how horrible his father was, but he did make a stern decision to be a godly and righteous king. Likewise, cast aside all of your crappy, chaotic, and messed-up family environment and begin to trust the Lord for your future. He will help you discover your inner kingdom identity and purpose that will transform your life and the lives of others.

Your kingdom purpose will not only make you unique but will also make you stand out from the rest of the crowd.

Takeaway Lessons from the Life of King Hezekiah

- Knowing your inner identity in Christ will make you original and you will also stand out from the rest of the crowd.
- Only those who have discovered their kingdom purpose will do what is right.
- God will fight on behalf of those who are willing to stand and fight for holiness, morality, and righteousness.

31
THE IDENTITY OF NEHEMIAH
Doing the Impossible

The story of Nehemiah reminds me of Legos. At one point or another, we had a certain fascination or addiction to playing with Legos. It is amazing as you can simply take these small colorful Lego pieces and construct something great. And your creativity of what you could possibly construct with these Logos is solely limited to you alone. And the story of Nehemiah does sound like a great Lego movie.

Here you have a character by the name of Nehemiah who builds an enormous wall out of thousands of boxes of Legos! Right? No! Nehemiah used the hands, feet, and body power of his fellow man, and the positive attitude of his fellow man to rebuild a massive wall that surrounded a huge city. It would have sounded like a great story for the kids before bedtime, but this is not a fairytale. It is a factual truth that God manifested himself through the willing hearts of the Israelites that were also as passionate as Nehemiah was in rebuilding the wall. And this chapter outlines how you can do what seems impossible as in the story of Nehemiah.

Knowing your God-given identity will result in you having a clear vision for your life, for your family, for your marriage, or for your business.

From a Servant-Slave to an Influential Leader

How does an individual go from being an unknow servant, to a very influential leader? The story of Nehemiah exemplifies this point in a profound way. You see, passion is a powerful motivator and when Nehemiah heard about the broken walls of Jerusalem and that his people were under great distress,

Nehemiah began to seek after the Lord. Because Nehemiah expressed his sincere passion and pain for the state of his city and his people before the king, the king asked him what he could do to help out. With boldness and wisdom from the Lord, Nehemiah asked the king for legal letters to travel through certain territories and for letters which also gave him permission to obtain enough timber for him to rebuild the gates on the wall and to rebuild the house of the Lord. The king granted him this and also sent military captains and horsemen with Nehemiah, for his protection.

The quick transition that Nehemiah experienced as he went from being a servant-slave to becoming an influential leader was truly remarkable. This similar type of transformation can occur with anyone, just as long as you have an inner conviction of passion for that very exact kingdom assignment that the Lord has created for you to fulfill on this earth.

People always want to be surrounded by those who know who they are, who know what they want to do, and who know where they are going in life.

Your Identity Is Magnetic

Nehemiah came to the Israelites as an outsider who was able to captivate the hearts of his fellow man and stirred within them the desire to rebuild the walls and the house of the Lord. The Israelites could sense Nehemiah's passion, and this attracted them to him like a magnet, creating a desire in them to support his vision.

Your identity is magnetic! But it is totally up to you to allow your passion for the thing which the Lord has called you to do on this earth to activate your God-given identity. And as you begin to operate in your kingdom calling, your natural passion for your calling will create a magnetic atmosphere that will attract others to you. And these individuals will be those that will eventually help or assist you in fulfilling your divine assignment on this earth.

Knowing and discovering your kingdom identity will allow you to know that you can do the impossible.

Your Gift Will Do the Impossible

The enemies of the Israelites mocked and threatened them while they were rebuilding the walls and the city, but a fifty-two day miracle occurred as they rebuilt the walls and the house of the Lord.[1] Because of Nehemiah's inner determination and strong leadership in organizing his people to rebuild the wall, the enemies and the surrounding nations were disheartened, seeing that God stood behind this phenomenon.

Your gift will do the impossible and will leave many people, especially your enemies, speechless. The key here is to fully allow the Lord to intervene in every matter, situation, circumstance, and deed that you do, whether great or small. Because whenever God takes ahold of something, then what may seem impossible to man becomes a testament and a wonder to everyone else. With that said, never despise or look down on your God-given gift or gifts. Often your gift may seem small or insignificant in the beginning phases of your life, but as you and I grow more in the knowledge of His Word and build a stronger intimacy with the Holy Spirit, then we will begin to witness that our gift can do the impossible.

Walking towards your destiny will require faith and warfare.

Fulfilling Your Purpose Will Require Faith and Spiritual Warfare

Because of the continual threats that came from the enemy, every Israelite held a construction tool in one hand and a weapon in the other. In similar manner, when it pertains to our purpose and calling, we should be going about our daily business to fulfill the assignment in our life and at the same time we need to be always ready to fight spiritual battles. The enemy of our soul will continually resist us, especially as we become very highly motivated in fulfilling the God-given assignment in our lives. And the more we stay focused on completing our kingdom assignment, the greater the opposition will be from the devil.

Your purpose will continually require faith and spiritual warfare. Why? Because your kingdom purpose is greater than you and greater than your abilities, and it will require you to continually trust the Lord until your dying breath. And because the enemy of your soul despises you and despises your purpose, he will continually initiate his demonic agents (often through people), to resist you and to hinder you from fulfilling your kingdom purpose. Always have faith in God and always be ready to fight the good fight with all of the heavenly weaponry that the Lord has equipped you with.

Those who choose to walk in their kingdom assignment will naturally attract the enemy of their soul, just like a magnet attracts anything metallic.

Do Not Compromise with Your Enemy

Sanballat sent out one of his messengers five times to inquire if Nehemiah would come to them so they could consult together, but Nehemiah knew that would jeopardize him or even get him killed. This is one of the oldest tricks up the devil's sleeves who will do whatever he can in order to leave you compromised. The challenge for us all is to make sure that we do not compromise with our enemy.

Those individuals who blindly or ignorantly went to the negotiation table with their enemy became victims of their own choosing, which sidetracked or detoured them from their kingdom assignment. Nehemiah knew that his enemies, Sanballat and Tobiah, desired evil for him, so he avoided their deadly trap of compromise. Likewise, many people will come out of the woodwork and try to hinder us, or even detour us from fulfilling our kingdom assignment. These individuals could even be from within our own family or even from within the circle of your friends. Stay focused on what God has called you to, and by doing so, you will not jeopardize or compromise your kingdom assignment.

Nehemiah once again reminds us that with God, and only with God, we can do the impossible, but this will require of you your passion and your inner determination. And as long as you do not compromise with the enemy of your soul and give in to the trickery or the bribery that he offers you, then you will be able to build and achieve great and mighty things in your life, in your family, in your marriage, in your business endeavors, or in your ministry.

As you continually and intimately stay connected with your Creator, your faith will begin to grow, and you will develop a belief for the impossible.

Takeaway Lessons from the Life of Nehemiah

- Your inner passion and convictions will direct you towards what you are called to do on this earth.
- As you function and operate in your kingdom assignment, you will then create a magnetic atmosphere which will attract others to you.
- Only, and I mean *only*, with God will you be able to do the impossible. Without Him, you and I are like a car without an engine.

32
THE IDENTITY OF
MORDECAI
Your Enemies and Critics Will Fall in Your Path

In the story of Mordecai, Mordecai reminds me of the cool kid on the block, while Haman is the neighborhood bully. And in this chapter, I focus on how your identity will give you boldness once you have discovered it. This chapter will also cover how critics and criticism is not something that you can avoid, because as long as you are pursuing your kingdom assignment, you will always have those who will challenge you, oppose you, mock you, laugh at you, ridicule you, and even discourage you. And finally, you will also learn the importance of abiding at the gate of Jesus since He is the gatekeeper of your kingdom identity and purpose.

The more time you spend with the King of kings the greater insight and revelation you will obtain for your kingdom assignment.

Sitting Within the King's Gate

It seemed that either Mordecai had too much time on his hands or was strategically used by God to be in the right place at the right time. Mordecai had a habit of sitting within the king's gate, and at one point, he overheard a conversation of the king's two eunuchs who were plotting to kill King Ahasuerus. This plot was made known to Queen Esther who eventually informed the king, and as a result, those two perpetrators were hanged on the gallows. When this event occurred, Mordecai's name and what he did was recorded in the book of the king's chronicles.[1]

This situation could have simply been described as being in the right place at the right time. Or did God have a greater purpose behind this matter? As time passed, King Ahasuerus could not sleep on one particular night, and he took the opportunity to have one of his servants read the book of chronicles in his presence. In this particular record, it was written how a man by the name of Mordecai had exposed an assassination plot against the king. When the king heard this record he said, "What honor or dignity has been bestowed on Mordecai for this?"[2] To the king's surprise, his servants said, "Nothing has been done for him."[3] Eventually, Mordecai was honored as if he were royalty where he wore one of the king's robes and he rode on the king's horse, and also received a royal crest which was placed on his head. And with all of this royal attire, Mordecai was paraded on the king's horse through the city square, and as he rode, these words were continually spoken, "Thus shall it be done to the man whom the king delights to honor."[4]

There is a powerful and a humorous point to this whole story. First, we should note that when we choose to sit or to invest our personal time within the gate of our King Jesus, we will receive fresh insight and revelation. Second, our deeds will be recorded in a *Book of Remembrance*.[5] Third, when the right time comes, our King will reward us openly. Fourth, your enemies will have no choice but to witness you being blessed and honored before many. This is exactly what happened to Mordecai when his enemy, Haman, had to give him honor as he rode him through the city square.

The fear of the Lord will make you bold and courageous as you walk in your kingdom purpose.

Being Bold and Fearless Before Others

Mordecai's boldness is a reminder that your inner identity and purpose will give you boldness, especially in times of criticism, oppression, opposition, or personal attacks from people. Because Mordecai knew his inner identity that God embedded into his spirit man, he was not afraid of Haman or his threats and was also willing to die for what he believed in.

The truth is that those who have understood or have discovered their kingdom identity no longer become afraid, intimidated, or distraught by those who try to oppress, suppress, or even criticize them. There was a time where I was somewhat intimidated by others and even unsure about my future, until I began to discover who I was in Christ and who I was through Christ. And when this maturity stage of my life occurred, I then became bolder.

Pride, a lying tongue, or a wicked heart will become like a virus to your purpose and calling.

Your Enemies and Critics Will Fall in Your Path

Haman despised Mordecai and erected gallows on which he thought he would have the pleasure of hanging Mordecai. But when Haman's evil plan was exposed, the king hung Haman and his whole family upon those same gallows that he intended for Mordecai.[6] God's justice and righteousness will eventually prevail. Just be patient and have faith in God who will fight off your enemies.

Your identity and purpose cannot fail because God does not fail. Now, through disobedience or lack of faith you could become a failure in life, but that does not mean that God failed you! Many Believers threw in a flag of surrender after their first encounter with criticism, which resulted in them detouring from their kingdom assignment. This often is a sign of spiritual immaturity, since critics and their distasteful criticism will follow you throughout your whole life. Why? Because for as long as you earnestly desire to walk in your purpose on this earth or to fulfill your kingdom vision, critics will naturally be attracted to you just like the bugs are attracted to the blue light. But the truth is, if you remain standing and focused on your kingdom assignment, then your enemies and critics will fall in your path, just like those bugs being zapped by a blue light.

You see, we cannot get rid of the Haman's in our life, but God can. And we also need to remember that God will give you the boldness you need to fulfill your destiny and that He will also give you great favor before great and influential individuals. Why? So, you can fulfill your calling on this earth.

Knowing who you are in Christ and through Christ will make you bold and courageous.

Takeaway Lessons from the Life of Mordecai

- Your identity will make you bold and fearless before your enemies.
- Your identity will position you in the right place, at the right time, and in the right season.
- Your identity will allow you to discern the tactics, the traps and the deception of your enemy.

33
THE IDENTITY OF ESTHER
Knowing Your Seasons

The story of Esther is very unique and it is also special. Throughout history, the Jewish people have been in numerous captivities and persecutions and were ruled by other nations. But in the story of Esther, she became a queen to a Gentile king.

We can definitely categorize this as a divine miracle and as intervention from God, which it was. But as we go further into the identity of Esther, we will uncover some powerful and applicable principles. Just for starters, one of the few requirements to qualify to be presented as a possible queen to King Ahasuerus was: You need to be young, beautiful, and a virgin.

I would like to strongly point out one of those three basic requirements and that is, you must be a *virgin*. In our modern-day culture, sexuality has been drastically redefined and continues to be restructured more and more into the perverted appetites of the individuals desire. If we choose to ignore the importance of our sexual purity and our sexual integrity, then we can easily forfeit our God-given identity and purpose on this earth. Many have already become victims to the destructive power of not having preserved their sexual identity to marriage only. No matter how beautiful Esther was, in accordance with Scripture, if she was not a virgin, she would have never become a queen and she would have never fulfilled her God-given assignment.

As you dive through the pages of this chapter, you will discover that you were specifically predestined to be born in this time and in this season. You will learn how your identity will attract specific people into your life, and you will discover the importance of fasting and why fasting is a key ingredient to your spiritual growth and for God opening unusual doors of favor and opportunities into your life. Also, you will learn how you will receive unusual favor. And finally, we will be discovering that you need to continually be in the presence of the Lord.

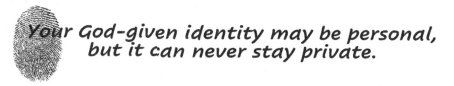

Your God-given identity may be personal, but it can never stay private.

You Were Born for Such a Time as This

One of the most profound statements in the Old Testament came from the lips of Mordecai when he addressed Esther: "Yet who knows whether you have come to the kingdom for *such* a time as this?"[1] Just in this one statement, Mordecai challenged Esther to seriously re-evaluate her God-given mission and why she became the chosen queen over the rest of the female candidates.

This text is not limited to Esther only but still speaks loudly until this day. I honestly believe that we all have at least one Mordecai in our life that God uses to remind us that we have been born for such a time as this. Yes, there is a divine reason why you were born in the twenty-first century and why you live where you live, or why you work where you work, or why you do what you do.

Remember, by discovering your inner identity, you will be able to discover your value and your worth. With the help of Mordecai, Esther began to understand how valuable she was and that her value was at its highest during the critical time where her people needed her intervention. And in like manner, people, society, your culture, and your generation need you more than you know. Why? Because God has divinely predestined for you to be born for "such a time as this."

Knowing your identity will help you to discover your gift, to refine your gift, and to release your gift!

Your Identity and Purpose Will Attract Specific People into Your Life

First came Mordecai who supported Esther in joining the king's beauty pageant. Second, came the king's eunuch who advised Esther on what the king preferred the most. And finally, Esther became a queen, and when a decree went forth to destroy her people the Jews, she used her influence before the king who eventually made another decree, and this resulted in the salvation of all the Jews. And until today, the Jews celebrate a holiday called Purim in remembrance of this historical event.

Your identity and purpose will attract specific people into your life, which is solely orchestrated by our heavenly Father. No one person can ever fulfill their God-given assignment on this earth without requiring the assistance, help, guidance, mentorship, and support of others. Just like God assigned specific individuals into the life of Esther, in like manner, God has already assigned specific people into your life who will help you to discover your identity and to help you to fulfill your kingdom purpose on this earth.

Purpose will keep you focused on how you can become a valuable asset, instead of a worthless liability in our society.

Your Identity and Purpose Will Give You Unusual Favor

We read, "And Esther obtained favor in the sight of all who saw her."[2] Something to powerfully note here is that Esther had favor with *all who saw her*. Wow! Right from start, Esther obtained favor from Hegai, who was the custodian of the women. Hegai gave Esther more beauty preparations than the rest of the young girls; he also provided choice maidservants, and he moved Esther to the best place in the house for women.

Oftentimes, we tend to blindside ourselves into thinking that others have it made, or some get very lucky or have great connections and that is why they are successful. That is not the case when it comes to the children of God. We do not operate under the assumption of luck but we operate under the favor of the Lord. God's favor is available to all of His children, and it is up to us to allow that unusual favor to work in our life and through our life. God does not have any favorites and God does not bless some more than others, since He does not operate under the principles of this worldly system.

It is imperative for every child of God to behold the truth that your identity and purpose will give you unusual favor before others, just like it did for Queen Esther. This divine favor is not intended to stroke your selfish ego, which would only result in pride, but is solely meant for you to operate and to be functionable in your kingdom assignment as you allow God to use you, to use your body, to use your potential, and to use your abilities for His kingdom purpose.

By discovering your identity and purpose, you then become a gift to this world.

Continually Bathe Yourself in the Presence of the Lord

Before Esther was presented before the king, she was prepared for twelve months. For six of those months, myrrh oils were rubbed into her skin and for the other six months it was precious perfumes. You can only image the sweet and pleasant aroma that transmitted from her body. This is a very powerful spiritual principle where each and every child of God needs to understand that we need to continually bathe in the presence of the Lord, so no matter where we go or what we do, His presence, peace, joy, love, grace, and anointing comes with us and flows from us.

Let us be real for a moment! All of us are used to our own body odor, but we do get uncomfortable and even nauseous from the odor of someone else, especially if the use of deodorant was neglected. This is another vital principle for us to grasp, that when the Lord's presence or His anointing is absent from our life, then we become like a spiritual stench in the nostrils of other people.

Your kingdom assignment will continually require you and I to be bathing in the presence of the Lord so that His anointing will never run dry in our life. And as we stay connected to the main source, who is Christ, then wherever we go, whatever we will do, and with whomever we will interact, God's presence will resonate from us and will create a transformational and a pleasant atmosphere. The identity of Esther underlines the notion that you and I need to know our divine seasons and for what our heavenly Father has called us to do on this earth.

Knowing your inner identity will give you the discernment to know your seasons.

Takeaway Lessons from the Life of Esther

- In the beginning, your identity will require a certain season of preparation as you spend time in the Lord's presence. And during that season, allow the Holy Spirit to rub His anointing into your spirit man.
- Your identity will take you from being an ordinary person and transform you into an influential individual.
- Your identity will give you boldness to stand before great, powerful, and influential individuals.

34
THE IDENTITY OF JOB
Never Give Up

How does someone qualify to be on Satan's most wanted hit list? What must one do in order to captivate the attention of Satan himself? And finally, what kind of life must you be living in order for the Lord to be personally bragging about you in the presence of Satan? Hopefully I got your attention with this opener!

Job's life story is yet another mind-blowing example of what takes place in the spiritual realm that is not visible to our natural eyes or disclosed to us in a way that we may understand it. And in this chapter, I will outline powerful principles about how your identity and purpose will be tested, must be tested, and how you cannot be exempt from various trials and tribulations in your lifetime on this earth.

Those who have discovered and understood their kingdom identity do not throw in a towel of surrender.

Never Give Up Because God Will Never Give Up on You

With the exception of Jesus, Job experienced some of the most painful and treacherous moments in life which occurred over a very short period of time. And one more important fact to keep in mind is that Satan personally attacked Job, just like he did through the temptation of Jesus. Often we have heard people say, "The devil is attacking me," or "Satan personally hates me," or "I must be number one on the devil's hit list." All that sounds cute, but the reality is far from the truth.

Satan has many demonic agents that he utilizes in oppressing and harassing humans, but for him to directly attack someone does not happen as often as we may think. My point is that Satan was really bothered by the fact of how blessed Job was and how much honor and reverence he gave to God. And it was Job's attitude and the integrity of his heart that grabbed Satan's attention. But what does that mean? The more you walk righteously before the Lord in accordance with His living Word, the more attention you will gain from the enemy of your soul.

I have had my fair share of dreadful seasons, and during one of those seasons I even wrote a book entitled: *When Life Is Full of It*. You may have experienced something similar to what Job has experienced but always remember not to give up, because God will never give up on you. We will experience plenty of suffering, unexpected tragedies, and numerous setbacks in life. You may be asking, "Why? I thought that we served a loving God who is there to protect us and to show us much grace and favor!" Yes, He does, but remember to look at the Bible correctly when it talks about God's children going through various trials and suffering on this earth. No matter what life may throw at you or whatever the enemy of your soul tries to do to you, never give up. And always know that your heavenly Father is always fighting on your behalf.

> *Your identity and calling will continually be challenged by others, especially by those closest to you.*

Your Identity Will Be Challenged by Your Family and Your Close Friends

I could only imagine how painful and difficult Job's situation was, but instead of being comforted by his wife, she had the nerve to say, "Curse God and die!"[1] And then for about fifteen chapters in a row, Job's closest friends criticized him by thinking that he had committed some kind of sin or disobedience towards God and that is why God was punishing him.

Do not you love that whenever you are going through one of the most challenging seasons of your life that those who are closest to you tend to become some of your greatest critics? Your identity will be challenged by your family members, close friends, and other fellow Christians, just like Job, Joseph, David, and others were. No one is exempt from this! Why? Because your identity is solely unique to you and only you are qualified to discover and to walk in your kingdom identity.

Here is a thought: have you ever criticized a professional athlete that made a wrong play or who was not able to score a point? We all have! It almost seems like a natural notion within every human being. That may be the fact, but the truth is that you and I are not that professional athlete and we do not possess their athletic skills and we are also not on the court playing ball. They are! This is also true when it comes to our kingdom identity that was given to us by God. And only we are able to walk in it and function in this identity while others in our life become those unsatisfied fans who will scream at us whenever we fall short, or fail, or make mistakes. Never forget, your identity will be challenged by your family, friends, coworkers, and fellow Believers.

Pain is a close friend to your kingdom assignment on this earth.

Your Identity Could Be Tested through a Severe Season of Painful Trials

From about 2010 to 2018, I and my wife went through some of the most severe trials of our life that seemed to be unbearable. But as I write this and reflect, it just seems like a vapor that came and went. Now, the battle scars are still there to remind us both about that long and exhausting season, but there is no pain left behind. So, what is the purpose of trials? And how do they complement my kingdom assignment? Let us take a look at the purpose of trials in our life:

- *Trials* make us strong and unbreakable.
- *Trials* keeps us focused on God who is the Author of our identity and purpose.
- *Trials* are like unique tools that God will utilize to make sure that we will not detour from our kingdom assignment.
- *Trials* purge our fleshly appetites which keep us distracted from our purpose.
- *Trials* sharpen our prayer life, increase our knowledge of the Word of God, and they also keep us spiritually alert.

My friend, no matter how painful or even heart stopping the trials or challenges you may have faced in your life are, always know this profound truth: our heavenly Father is more concerned for our well-being and for us fulfilling our kingdom assignment on this earth and He will not allow any trial or tragedy to stand in our way. As much as Job's suffering may have seemed unbearable, at the end of it all, God still blessed him with a double portion. And in like manner, if we do not lose heart and never give up, then we will see greater and more prosperous days ahead of us.

Never give up! Never surrender! Your kingdom calling is way too valuable.

Takeaway Lessons from the Life of Job

- Knowing your identity and purpose will give you the motivation and the endurance to not give up.
- If you notice that you are not being challenged or criticized by your family members, by your friends, or by those who know you, then you need to have a serious evaluation on whether you are walking in your kingdom calling.
- Those who choose to function in their kingdom assignment and purpose will go through numerous trials that will test you, that will shape you, and will form you into the needed vessel that God can use.

35
THE IDENTITY OF DANIEL
What Is on the Menu? Your Identity!

In the Bible, there is nobody that functioned to their fullest capacity like Daniel did as a political advisor. When it comes to politics or the political sphere, Christians get divisive, contentious, and have their personal opinions on whether Believers need to get involved in the political sphere or simply stay out of it.

The book of Daniel is often credited to be a book that is full of prophecies and is also often referenced by the teachers and scholars who teach prophecy. That may be true, but we cannot ignore that Daniel's role and the function was heavily involved in the political sphere where he spent much of his life as the primary advisor to four separate kings.

The identity of Daniel is truly fascinating as he was among those taken into captivity, then forced to study the language, the culture and the customs of the Babylonians, and he eventually become a very influential person to the gentile kings. Daniel was also hated and despised by his fellow political advisors which resulted in them convincing the king to make an anti-Christian law, as I would like to call it, that forbade Daniel to pray. And when he violated this law, he ended up on the lion's menu.

In this particular chapter, you will embark on a unique kingdom assignment that God has anointed, and has appointed some to be functioning in, and that is the political sphere. You will also take away valuable lessons on why it is imperative for you to separate yourself from the appetites of this world. And finally, you will also discover that your identity will always be on the devil's menu, because he is a hungry lion always looking for whom he may devour.

Knowing your inner identity will help you to plan your way (or envision it), and as you do, God will direct your steps.

Separate Yourself from the Appetites of This World

Daniel made a bold choice to not partake of the king's table and all of the delicacies that were offered on it. He also chose to not partake of the wine. By doing this, it became very evident to the chief of the eunuchs that Daniel and his three Hebrew friends looked healthier and eventually became more knowledgeable, more skilled, and obtained more wisdom then the rest of their peers.

The choice of separating yourself from the appetites of this world is not a suggestion but a strong proposition. Those who foolishly think that they can indulge themselves with worldly appetites and also be able to function in their kingdom assignment are only fooling themselves. Yes, in some capacity you can still function in your calling, because the gift of God is irrevocable,[1] but those who try to live a double lifestyle fall under this condemnation as it is written in the book of Revelation, "So then, because you are lukewarm, and neither cold nor hot, I will vomit you out of My mouth."[2]

Many have been lured away with the appetites of this world and then they begin to wonder why they do not know their God-given identity or why they are not successful in their kingdom assignment. The choice that Daniel and his three friends made was not easy, since they could've jeopardized their own lives, but they made a stern decision not to partake from the king's table and likewise we should not partake from the devils table which may seem very appetizing. When you choose to separate yourself from the appetites of this world, you then begin to partake of the table of the Lord, which will feed your faith and will give you the spiritual food needed to fulfill your purpose on this earth.

Never limit or despise your own identity and purpose.

Called to the Political Sphere of Influence

Daniel fulfilled one of the greatest political roles in the Bible, and the Lord used him through four separate administrations (four kings). Like never before in the history of our country, we have witnessed so many divisions in politics. And yes, I am talking about the presidency of Donald Trump. But what is most tragic of all is how the body of Christ became divided during the election and especially after the election. The tragedy here is that many Christians have set aside their kingdom and biblical identity and have begun to wear the color red or the color blue and have become a political spokesperson instead of focusing on the King and on His kingdom mandate.

One big issue today is that we have too much politics in the church and not enough kingdom goals. Our preachers have turned into politicians and political advocates instead of kingdom visionaries. And much of our focus has been on the latest Donald Trump tweets, instead of focusing on the Holy Spirit, who has been working overtime with His inner tweets towards our hearts that we have been ignoring.

Daniel fulfilled a key role as a political advisor, and even as a spiritual advisor, to four different kings. And his unique kingdom assignment has also played a key role in the deliverance of his own people who were set free after seventy years of captivity. I strongly believe that God has called certain individuals from the body of Christ to be a type of Daniel in the political sphere. And as I write this, one of these individuals also happens to be my own pastor, Jentezen Franklin. From time to time, during Sunday or Wednesday services, he would partially share on his role and function as one of the spiritual advisors to President Donald Trump. He does not share any specific details but does boldly say how privileged and honored he is that the Lord has entrusted him in this specific sphere of influence. And if you believe that the Lord has called you into the political sphere, then like never before we need credible and Godly individuals like Daniel who the Lord can use powerfully in order to advance His kingdom purpose on this earth.

Only those who function in their God-given purpose will be attacked, criticized, opposed, and even persecuted.

Fasting Is an Essential Ingredient for Fulfilling Your Kingdom Assignment

You may have heard of the twenty-one-day Daniel Fast! It is so named because Daniel prayed and fasted for twenty-one days, and on the twenty first day of his fast, the angel Gabriel came to answer his prayers. When it comes to fasting, it seems that quite a few Christian folks misunderstand the purpose of fasting or totally have the wrong theological understand of why fasting is such an essential ingredient for helping us to fulfill our kingdom assignment on this earth.

Throughout the Bible, we have many scriptural references to fasting, including the forty-day fast of Jesus Himself. When it comes to fasting, it is not merely abstaining from food, but laying aside the desire of your fleshly appetites to increase your inner hunger for the Lord and for His perfect will for your life. The inner hunger that was seen in Daniel got the attention of heaven, which resulted in a heavenly messenger who brought forth great news to him of the freedom and liberation that was going to occur for the Israelites.

Additionally, Jesus once said, "However, this kind does not go out except by prayer and fasting."[3] Here He was referring to casting out strong demons. Yes, fasting is not only needed in your spiritual walk with the Lord, but it is essential in helping you to fulfill your kingdom assignment and calling.

Your purpose will always be targeted by the devil.

What's on the Menu? Your Identity!

We may be on the devil's menu, but we should not end up on his plate! Daniel's enemies thought that they came up with the greatest plan to finally get rid of their nemesis. But as the story goes, Daniel's name ended up on the menu, but never on the plate of the lions. The only ones who ended up on the lion's dinner plate were Daniel's enemies and their family members.

After reading and hearing the same biblical stories repeatedly, like Daniel in the lion's den, David killing Goliath, Peter walking on water, or the favorite one of all, when Jonah was swallowed by a great fish, we could become dangerously immune to the truthfulness of these powerful and supernatural things that God did and begin to look at them as just great stories and nothing more. In a similar context, we could also become passive towards the great miracles that have occurred in our own personal life. For Daniel, his situation was as real as it gets, and I doubt that he had a smirk on his face when he saw the hungry lions approaching him.

One thing we should never be ignorant to is that our enemies and the enemy of our soul is continually walking around like a bloodthirsty lion, looking to whom he may devour. Our God-given identity and purpose will always be under attack and will often be criticized. And yes, your identity and kingdom assignment will be on the devil's menu, but it is up to us to make sure that they never end up on his dinner plate!

Knowing your kingdom identity will make you a risk taker, and not a pew warmer.

Takeaway Lessons from the Life of Daniel

- Many Believers end up on the lion's menu. Why? Because they choose to live a risk-free life
- You will never know if you were called to influence great individuals until you discover your God-given identity.
- Knowing your purpose will continually challenge you to abstain from the appetites of this world.

136

36
THE IDENTITY OF SHADRACH, MESHACH, AND ABED-NEGO
Are You Fireproof?

The first chapter of the book of Daniel outlines how the rulers of this world work and operate through their strategic craftiness. Nebuchadnezzar, the king of Babylon, is symbolic to the authoritative, influential, and powerful individuals in our modern-day world. When he took the Israelites captive, he ordered his master of the eunuchs to capture young men who had no blemish, were good looking, were gifted in all wisdom, possessed knowledge and quick understanding, and who had the ability to serve in the king's palace.[1]

As you carefully review the above qualifications that king Nebuchadnezzar gave, you would quickly understand that the king was searching for the best of the best. This is exactly what we are tragically observing in our society today, where we are seeing more and more very talented, gifted, skilled, knowledgeable, and innovative individuals from within the younger generation that are being sucked into the worldly vacuum where their God-given potential and gifts are being utilized towards worldly and demonic propaganda. In other words, the devil is not interested in leftovers or in average people, but he steals the cream of the crop.

In this chapter, I will address what role the academia is fulfilling in today's society. And most importantly, I will cover why your purpose and kingdom assignment need to be fireproof.

In order for you to successfully walk in your kingdom calling, you need to continually abide in the fear of the Lord.

Is Academia a Tool or a Powerful Weapon?

A recent survey said that Christian youth who have not been strongly grounded in the Word of God and in their faith, within their first year or so of college, about eighty-five percent of them will fall away from their faith and stop attending church. Now these are some heart-breaking statistics. But does it have to be so? Absolutely not!

Is academia a tool or a powerful weapon? This question is not meant to be humorous or even politically correct, but it is stated as a cautionary evaluation. The three Hebrew teenagers who were taken into Babylonian captivity were taught the language and literature of the Chaldeans and they were also offered the king's delicacies and wine, which they declined.[2] These Hebrew friends were, in a sense, forced to study and to learn the language and literature of a foreign culture and submit to the authority that they were under. With that said, they did not surrender their inner convictions and stayed true to who they were and continued to abide in the fear of the Lord.

Academia is supposed to be a tool and a place for developing the younger generation, but in the past two decades or so, these institutions have become propaganda machines, which have switched from teaching to indoctrinating. Yes, this is a bold statement on my part, but having served and mentored the younger generation for so many years, as a father of three, and as a kingdom ambassador, I would be doing you a disfavor if I did not address this vital issue.

I fervently believe that we need more kingdom minded individuals who could carry the mantle in the sphere of academia, whether they are teachers, principals, or other influential personnel. We desperately need those who have a kingdom calling to be in the arena of academia, as they would become the bright beacons of light.

Knowing your identity will help you to choose your friends in accordance with your destiny and purpose.

Your Purpose and Kingdom Assignment Need to Be Fireproof

These three young and courageous Hebrews were risking their life by not bowing down to the golden idol. But one thing for sure was that the fire they carried inside of them was much greater than the fire that burned from within the fiery furnace. And the serious question that we all need to ask ourselves is, "Is my purpose and kingdom assignment fireproof?"

Honestly, there is no simple way of stating this, but the truth of the matter is that your kingdom purpose and assignment on this earth must be fireproof. In other words, it must be tested through fiery trials, which I have outlined in more details in Chapter thirty-four "The Identity of Job." You see, the inner fire that we carry, the fire of the Holy Spirit, needs to be stronger than any demonic fire that will resist you or try to resist your kingdom assignment.

In recent years, like never before, we are witnessing so many prominent Christian leaders falling away from the faith or we are hearing of numerous stories where pastors or church leaders dropped out of ministry because they have simply burnt out and got too tired. This is very tragic and nothing that we should take lightly. These three young Hebrew friends exemplified the true power of God that was upon them, which also became a very powerful testimony before the secular king who eventually reversed his new decree and said that whoever does not worship the God of these Hebrews will be thrown into the fiery furnace.

The bold stance that Shadrach, Meshach, and Abed-Nego took underlines the importance of why we need to be assured of our inner identity and purpose on this earth. Also, I would like to challenge and encourage everyone who is currently in academia as a student or as a teacher that God does have a great plan for you, but you should not submit or cave in to the modern-day socialistic agenda that is so evident in the sphere of academia. When you choose to resist or oppose the worldly philosophy that is anti-God, anti-Bible, or anti-Christian, then you will be persecuted and feel like the fiery breath of hell is breathing at you, but if you remain faithful, then God will manifest Himself in you and through you in a very powerful way. And as a result, your testimony will become even greater before others.

The bold stance of these three friends should be encouraging for the younger generation, especially if you are still studying in academia. Much good comes from the academic sphere, but much evil and destruction are also spewing through the teachers, professors, and through academic literature. And the kingdom position that these three young Hebrews took should be a role model for all students, as they have exemplified that the God that lives inside of you is greater than any demonic or demoralizing theology that is rampant in our modern-day culture.

Modern-day culture will teach you to blend in, while your inner identity and purpose will challenge you to stand out.

Takeaway Lessons from the Life of Shadrach, Meshach, and Abed-Nego

- Your identity and purpose will not prevent you from going through fiery trials, but will preserve you, just as long as you place your trust in the Lord.
- Obtaining knowledge and education is great but walking in the fear of the Lord supersedes everything.
- Fiery trials are tools to test the authenticity and the credibility of your God-given identity.

37
THE IDENTITY OF JONAH
God Is Not in the Business of Controlling You or Patrolling You but Only of Guiding You

The Book of Jonah is one of the shortest chapters in the Old Testament but it contains some of the most powerful life lessons as it pertains to our identity and purpose. Jonah was just an ordinary prophet, but he was given an extraordinary kingdom assignment that he chose to disobey God with.

Whether Jonah had a bad day, or some personal family issues, or even a hatred towards the Ninevites, he does exemplify many Christians today. We sometimes behave like immature children and may think that our heavenly Father is trying to control or patrol our life on earth. But we may not realize that His heart's desire is to guide us every day of our life so we can successfully fulfill our kingdom assignment.

Let us take our own whale ride through this adventurous chapter and you will discover that you may temporarily run away from your purpose on this earth, but God has a way of bringing you back into your spiritual alignment. Also, we need to take full responsibility for our life and for our kingdom assignment on this earth. And finally, our assignment and purpose will always involve serving others. There is no exception to this kingdom principle!

> *Disobedience to your original assignment could result in various unpleasant seasons of your life.*

One Whale of a Ride

No pun intended! (Or maybe it was!) We have all been on our own type of whale rides which were not very pleasant. Often we get carried away by pointing a finger at the devil, thinking that it is him who is creating the turbulent storms in our life, without possibly considering that it might be our own disobedience to God or to His will for our lives. Wisdom teaches us to first re-evaluate our lives, our hearts, and our choices through prayer and even fasting, and then with a sound mind and an open heart we will be able to obtain insight from the Holy Spirit to what we need to do in our current stormy season. You may have to repent of or change a few things in your life or just continue to trust in the Lord for your breakthrough.

Our heavenly Father is not in the business of creating storms just for the sake of His amusement in heaven, but there are many Believers who still believe that God specifically orchestrates these storms in order to teach us a lesson or to break us. When I read the living Word of God it states, "For I know the thoughts that I think toward you, says the Lord, thoughts of peace and not of evil, to give you a future and a hope."[1] So, if you do not want to go through unnecessary storms or whale rides, then learn how to walk in obedience to His Word and in His perfect will for your life.

Obedience is a key component to you successfully fulfilling your kingdom purpose.

You Can Run but You Cannot Hide

Jonah thought that he had a clever plan by trying to outsmart God, but eventually he realized the hard truth. One powerful truth that I have discovered in my life is that my God-given purpose and assignment on this earth is not strictly limited to me alone but involves and affects many others. Let us take a look at what occurred because of Jonah's disobedience to God:

- God sent a great wind in the sea.
- The mariners were afraid.
- Every person cried out to his own god.
- They threw cargo into the sea to lighten the weight.
- Everyone's life was in jeopardy.

Here comes the best part! While all of the above was taking place, Jonah was having a slumber party below the deck like nothing was happening. A few more insightful points to consider from this situation:

- Your disobedience to God's will for your life, will make you fall spiritually asleep.
- While others around you are suffering, confused, displaced, or seeking out false gods, you are selfishly only concerned for your own well-being.
- While you are delaying your kingdom assignment, you will potentially suffer financial loss of wealth that was meant for you and

your family, and for your kingdom assignment. While Jonah slept, the crew threw much cargo overboard to increase their chances of survival.

You could try to run away from God, but His love and passion for you is so great that He will not be able to hold back His affection towards you, and He will do everything that He can to draw you back to Himself, to His presence, and to His perfect will that He has predestined for you on this earth. Disobedience will make you run and hide from God, just like Adam and Eve did, but your obedience to Him will make you run into His loving arms.

Identity is just like salt. It is supposed to add flavor to your life and to the life of others.

Take Full Responsibility for Your Life, for Your Purpose, and for Your Assignment

The captain of the boat eventually caught Jonah sleeping and made this interesting remark, "What do you mean, sleeper?"[2] I am sure that was a type of a cursing statement back in the day, but I will not try to make a doctrine out of this. Anyway, the captain was furious that everyone on the boat was doing whatever they could to keep themselves alive and to prevent the boat from sinking while Jonah was snoozing away.

Eventually, Jonah spoke the whole truth to his fellow shipmates and even admitted that the treacherous storm was his fault because he disobeyed God. Once Jonah took full responsibility for his disobedience towards God, he took a bold step by telling the others on the boat that they needed to throw him overboard and the storm would cease. That is exactly what they did and that is exactly what happened with the storm.

We can always play the blame game, but that can only go so far and for so long. Eventually you will have your own reality check moment when you will need to take full responsibility for your life, for your purpose, and for your kingdom assignment. And when you do, your life will be blessed, and you will also become a blessing to others.

Purpose is like a healthy supplement for your life. Discover your purpose early, so you can live a stress-free life.

143

Your Assignment Will Always Consist of Serving Others

Even after Jonah's chaotic boat ride and three days in the belly of the fish, he still became angry with the Lord for not destroying Nineveh and its people. One more important lesson that we can take away from Jonah, is that his heart was not in proper spiritual alignment. He was called to be a prophet and a mouthpiece of the Lord, but even after he preached repentance to the Ninevites, he was not interested in their salvation, but in their destruction. Remember, our assignment will always involve serving others in one way or another and serving people is one of the toughest things that anyone can do, because they all come wrapped in different packages and you never know what to expect.

Servanthood is a great privilege, but it does come with a price tag. Whether you offer a service or a product, at the other end will always be a client that is a human being and who needs to be treated as a human being. When it comes to your kingdom assignment, serving others is not an option or a cute suggestion, but a must since God's business is the business of souls. And I like how one of my spiritual mentors often says, "I'm commanded by God to love and to serve everyone, but I'm not obligated to become their friend."

Every individual is born with their unique kingdom manual and it is up to you to discover and to understand what God has written about you in your manual of life.

Your Assignment and Purpose Have a Specific Function

God only had Jonah in mind to go preach to Nineveh, no one else. So, when Jonah decided to disobey God by running away from his original assignment, God still orchestrated events and situations by trying to bring him back into alignment and to an understanding of his assignment. In like manner, your assignment and purpose is solely designated to you and to you alone, and God will do everything He can to help you to bring everything into its alignment to fulfill that assignment, even if He has to humble you, break you, or even close specific doors.

Whenever a manufacturer designs a specific product, they put certain rules and regulations into place concerning that specific product. For example, a car manufacturer strictly states that you can only put unleaded gasoline or diesel fuel into each specific vehicle. But you as the owner of that vehicle can decide otherwise. If you think it is too expensive to fill your car with fuel, you can decide to put water into your tank, or apple juice, or another liquid. Of course, there will be some major consequences such as the car will now malfunction, breakdown, or you could even ruin the whole engine.

In a similar way, our heavenly Father, who is also our Creator, has already specifically designed within each and every single one of us a specific purpose and function, but when we decide to do something else in our life or with our life or with our potential, then things begin to malfunction in our life. And because of this, we become discouraged, devastated, and even angry at God.

The story of Jonah may seem like a great Sunday school lesson, but the kingdom principles that are sketched out for us in this short chapter are profound. Jonah taught us that we could try to run away from our kingdom assignment, but our heavenly Father is way too gracious to leave us alone, and He still places us back onto the right path, if we desire it. Also, Jonah teaches us the valuable lesson that we need to take full responsibility of our lives, our actions, our daily choices, and our submission to the Lord for His will to be done in us and through us.

Do not get angry or upset with God whenever He corrects you since it is only His loving desire to bring you into the original alignment of your purpose on this earth.

Takeaway Lessons from the Life of Jonah

- Your kingdom calling was uniquely engraved into your spiritual DNA, which makes you the only qualified candidate to fulfill it.
- You can bury your identity, or hide it, or even throw it away. Your identity is always present within you, but it is solely up to you whether you walk in your identity or not.
- Those who do not desire to serve others have not discovered or understood their kingdom purpose. Why? Because your kingdom purpose will always include serving others.

38
THE IDENTITY OF JOHN THE BAPTIST
Fully Sold Out

John the Baptist received one of the greatest compliments from Jesus when He said, "For I say to you, among those born of women there is not a greater prophet than John the Baptist."[1] I guess the big and curious question is, what is Jesus saying about you and I?

John the Baptist's family background is very impressive to say the least, and just like Moses' parents, we once again witness the crucial importance of what role parents fulfill in the kingdom assignment and purpose of their child. Throughout this chapter you will discover why your assignment is unusual to you, and because of this you will have plenty of doubtful moments wondering if your calling was from God or if it was just your ambitious imagination.

Do not get confused, discouraged, or sidetracked by the uniqueness of your gift and your calling, since God never makes mistakes.

An Unusual Individual with an Unusual Assignment

The Bible describes the ministry name of John the Baptist as "The Voice of One Crying in the Wilderness."[2] And instead of him wearing a nice-looking priestly robe, he wore camel's hair with a leather belt around his waist. And instead of enjoying the priestly table, he ate locusts and honey. In other words, this preacher looked like a wild caveman with some extremely wild breath. Just think about it!

Yes, John the Baptist preached repentance and baptized anyone who desired it, but his main assignment was to prepare the way for Jesus, as he once said, "There comes One after me who is mightier than I, whose sandal strap I am not worthy to stoop down and loose."[3] What does this mean for you and I? Sometimes we get too carried away by observing or analyzing the life or the kingdom assignment of other Believers and we attempt to reflect their assignment and purpose in our own, which could result in much discouragement.

There was a lengthy season when I observed great men and women of God and what they were doing for God's kingdom, but when I looked back into my own mirror, I got the hardcore reality check that what I was doing or what I was seeing seemed very little and insignificant. These were during my early years of youth ministry. But by God's grace and through much prayer, I began to see the bigger picture for my life and for my purpose on the earth. In other words, I discovered how unique I was and that my assignment and calling was unusual. Many years later, I still function in the same revelation. Remember, you are unusual, and your kingdom assignment is uniquely unusual to you.

Sooner or later you will encounter a spiritual identity crisis and begin to doubt your purpose and calling, but do not be discouraged, every child of God experiences similar spiritual symptoms.

Everyone Will Eventually Have a Moment of Doubt about Their Purpose

John the Baptist was privileged to introduce Jesus and His ministry to mankind. But when John was imprisoned, he began to doubt his original purpose and assignment, and one day while in prison, he sent two of his disciples to Jesus with this question, "Are You the Coming One, or do we look for another?"[4] This particular moment in John the Baptist's life is of no exception, since everyone at one point or another will have a moment of doubt about their purpose.

Absolutely no one is exempt from having fearful or doubtful moments about their kingdom assignment and purpose. These doubtful moments have no limitations or boundaries! Why? Simply because we are human beings who are full of insecurity, doubt, fear, and lack of insight for God's full purpose and plan for our lives. If only all of the biblical characters would have fully known God's detailed will for their life, then we would have read the Bible in a whole different way, but that is not how it works. Remember, for as long as we have these moments of doubt, this then becomes another great opportunity for us to trust and to rely even more on our heavenly Father, and for Him to continue to guide us through our spiritual growth process. And this growth process will continue until our dying breath on this earth.

Knowing your kingdom identity will keep you disciplined, focused, and full of passion.

Your Assignment Could Be Vital to Prepare the Way for the Next Great Reformation

Every Elijah will have an Elisha. Every Jonathan will have a King David. Every Mordecai will have an Esther. And every John the Baptist will have a Jesus. This neither makes that individual's assignment more special, nor more burdensome. We do not choose our kingdom assignment, but our heavenly Father does. But we do have a choice whether we will fulfill this kingdom assignment or not!

Before I moved my family to the state of Georgia, I sincerely believed for many years that God would manifest a great revival in the New England region of America, and I still do. But now I no longer live there! One takeaway lesson from this is that God will use us for a specific season and for a specific purpose and for a specific assignment, and then He will direct us to other things. For as long as we have been obedient to Him in that particular season, then we have accomplished our kingdom assignment since God already has someone else in mind to continue where we have left off.

This kingdom principle is so essential for us all to understand because many are still holding onto their baton while the Lord has many times prompted that particular individual to pass the baton to the next runner. This is, this has, and this continues to be a cancerous issue in the body of Christ. We have pastors who have not had a fresh revelation or vison for their local church in years but are still holding onto their position as a senior pastor. We have church leaders who have not seen growth or who are no longer relevant in their particular ministry, but God forbid that you tell them to pass on that baton lest they chew

148

you out. And over the years, I have also observed and heard of numerous frustrations from the younger generation that their local church only has senior or older leaders who are not interested in having younger leaders in leadership positions. So, if your church or your ministry is not growing or becoming more influential, then this could be a spiritual diagnosis that it is time for you to move on and to pass on the baton to someone else.

If we could learn a powerful lesson from the life of John the Baptist it would be that he was not power hungry, position focused, or starstruck with status. He served the people faithfully, but deep inside he knew that he was preparing a way from someone that was much greater than he was. This is a true sign of humility from someone who understood that their kingdom assignment was preparing the way for someone else who would usher in a great reformation and revival.

We can also reference the calling and purpose of John the Baptist as an intercessory prayer warrior. God has chosen and appointed specific Believers to stand in the gap and to intercede on behalf of the body of Christ and God will use them as powerful weapons. The body of Christ can definitely use more of those who carry a similar mantle as John the Baptist. With that said, you and I need to be individuals who are fully sold out to God's will and purpose for our lives.

The day you discover your God-given identity and purpose will be the day when you will tune out all of the noise around you, and tune in more to the voice of God.

Takeaway Lessons from the Life of John the Baptist

- God's will for your life is perfect, but you are not. So, we will have plenty of moments of doubt as we function in our kingdom calling.
- History makers are those who have fully surrendered their lives to the Lord in order to fulfill His perfect will.
- Only those who have discovered and understood their God-given identity become fully sold out to the work of the Lord.

39
THE IDENTITY OF VIRGIN MARY
Keep Your Vessel Pure

When we were growing up, it was normal for us to have a unique nickname given to us either by our parents, one of our siblings, by our friends, or maybe by one of our classmates. Nicknames carry special characteristics that tend to identify, describe, or outline a specific individual in a humorous way.

Whether you liked your given nickname or whether you despised it, sometimes it is very difficult for us to simply cast it aside, since that particular nickname exemplifies a specific individual. And in the case of Mary, the biological mother of Jesus, the Bible described her in the following manner: "The virgin's name was Mary."[1] There is absolutely nothing wrong with the Bible describing her as a virgin since she was, but more than two thousand years later she is still referred to as the Virgin Mary, especially in Catholicism.

In this particular chapter I want to take a whole different approach as I outline the identity of the Virgin Mary by focusing more on why her so-called nickname of *Virgin Mary* is vital and how it speaks loudly to our modern-day sexually immoral culture. A question that we all need to seriously consider as we read this whole chapter is, "What role or purpose does my virginity, or my sexual purity play in my divine assignment and purpose on this earth?"

Do not deprive the world and humanity from discovering who you are and what untapped potential lays within you.

A Sexual Revolution

In our modern-day culture, there is an explosion in the sexual revolution, where the word *virgin* or *virginity* is becoming extinct in the lexicon. When I was single and shared with others that I was still a virgin, my classmates, co-workers, and other peers laughed at me and some even called me gay.

The sexual revolution that keeps on growing in our culture places much emphasis on freedom, experimentation, and the appetite for trying something unusual. Like never before, there are so many different sexual orientations and names that one needs to pull out a dictionary in order to understand their meanings and their definitions.

When God created Adam and Eve, He limited the genders to only two and gave a command to keep any sexual relations or activities within marriage. And with His divine wisdom, He solely restricted any sexual or attractive preferences towards the opposite sex and not towards the same gender. And when it comes to this demoralizing sexual revolution, we as children of God need to always go back to the original source. As soon as we submit to the demonic notion that it was God who created someone to have attractions or sexual interests towards the same gender or for someone to choose what gender they best prefer for themselves, then we begin to play with serious fire.

The Word of God is plain and clear when it comes to explaining sexuality or gender identity. It is one thing when people who do not know Christ or those who are struggling with their identity are facing confusion in the area of sexuality or gender identity, but it is very tragic when we see this same confusion taking place amongst those who call themselves Christians.

You are not a mistake and God did not purposely generate confusion in your hormones or in your human DNA. Our God is a perfect God who makes everything perfect, but our nemesis, the devil, is always looking for ways and opportunities on how to distort, disrupt, confuse, complicate, and to deconstruct God's original masterpiece. So, no matter what our current sexual revolution is advocating, God's Word will never change.

Knowing your calling and purpose will challenge you to continually live a life of holiness and purity.

Keep Your Vessel Pure

In Thessalonians we read a powerful statement as it relates to sexual purity, "It is God's will that you be sanctified: that you should avoid sexual immorality; that each of you should learn to control your own body in a way that is holy and honorable, not in passionate lust like the pagans, who do not know God."[2]

151

The Bible is full of direct references and numerous illustrations about our sexual purity and that we need to keep our vessel pure and undefiled. The Bible is also full of examples of many different types of things that are considered sin or sinful, but Apostle Paul made an interesting remark in reference to our sexuality when he said, "Flee sexual immorality. Every sin that a man does is outside the body, but he who commits sexual immorality sins against his own body."[3]

This is a profound distinction that sexual immorality is a direct sin against your own physical body! This may be why we have so many horrific sexually transmitted diseases, HIV being the deadliest of all. As I have mentioned earlier, in this particular chapter I wanted to outline a different characteristic quality from the life of the Virgin Mary that covers the area of virginity, sexual purity, and preserving your sexuality for marriage and for marriage only.

It may not be popular to talk about this divine gift of sexuality that God has embedded into our human body, but if God's children do not shed the biblical viewpoint to this crucial subject, then the world will definitely share its own deadly ideology. Do seriously consider that your sexual purity and integrity plays a vital role in your kingdom calling and assignment. Do not forfeit your purpose on this earth over a quick one-night stand. Remember, the Virgin Mary was not chosen by God because of her good looks, but because she carried an exceptional measure of purity in her heart and in her life.

Never compare yourself to others since your God-given identity and kingdom assignment is solely unique to you.

Takeaway Lessons from the Life of Mary

- Your identity and calling cannot be separated from your sexual identity.
- Many have aborted their kingdom purpose because they did not live a sexually pure life. Keeping your vessel pure is not a suggestion, but a commandment from God.
- Your identity and your purpose are relevant to your sexual purity more than you could even comprehend.

40
THE IDENTITY OF APOSTLE THOMAS
How Is This Conceivable?

Here is a hypothetical conversation that we could have had with the Apostle Thomas:

"Hey Thomas, how's life?"
"I don't know!"
"Thomas, how are you doing?"
"Not sure!"
"Thomas, what are your goals for life?"
"I don't know!"
"Hey Thomas, do you know your kingdom identity?"
"What's that?"

And with these sarcastic questions, I want to begin this chapter by outlining the identity of "doubting Thomas" who resembles hundreds of millions of people around the world.

Here we have one of the chosen disciples of Jesus, who lost hope and was full of despair after the death of Jesus, and even when he heard a credible testimony that Jesus was alive, he still doubted it as we see in the following passage: "The other disciples therefore said to him, 'We have seen the Lord.' So he said to them, 'Unless I see in His hands the print of the nails, and put my finger into the print of the nails, and put my hand into His side, I will not believe.'"[1]

Before we dare to judge Apostle Thomas, we should first analyze ourselves because we often have also doubted the Lord in our personal life. In this chapter, I point out that we all have plenty of moments of doubt, but if we allow the Word of God to become rhema (God's Word spoken to you) in our spirit man, then this word will become conceived inside of us, which will give birth to who we are in Christ and to our kingdom purpose and calling on this earth.

Critics are not your enemies, but only a confirmation for you to continue to move forward in your kingdom calling.

Do Not Doubt Your Purpose and Calling

Doubt never had too many friends! Doubt never had healthy relationships! Doubt always fears the future and often remembers the past. Doubt could honestly sabotage your purpose and destiny. And doubt even doubts itself!

Apostle Thomas falls into the same group category as Peter and Judas Iscariot, who all three illustrate a high caliber of spiritual identity crisis while walking alongside the Son of God. In other words, it is very possible for an individual to regularly attend church, to read the Bible, and to pray, but still struggle inwardly with doubt of who they are in Christ and who they are through Christ.

The identity of Apostle Thomas teaches us all that fear and doubt will taunt you, especially during the most vulnerable seasons of your life, which could be called your wilderness, your transition, or a time when you feel that God is not listening. And it is during these dire moments that fear and doubt team up as one hits you from the right side, and the other hits you from the left.

It is alright if you doubt your calling or purpose, just as I did during some of my most vulnerable seasons, but when you grab ahold of Jesus, just like doubting Thomas did, then our inner faith will receive a divine boost to keep on moving forward knowing that God is in control of your life and He knows exactly what He is doing and where He is leading you to.

The more of God's word becomes alive in your heart and in your spirit man, the clearer your kingdom assignment becomes to you.

How Is This Conceivable?

Can this be possible? Can this really be true? How in the world could this ever happen? No matter how doubtfully you gaze upon your life and upon your purpose and calling, it is essential for you to first, by faith, believe, or believe that your life has purpose, and that you were born for a purpose to fulfill a specific purpose. When this revelation is conceived in your spirit man and in your subconscious, then this truth becomes conceivable.

When the rhema word becomes conceivable in you, then you begin to believe in that word. The word *conceive* is also applied towards a woman that wants to get pregnant, and based on her cycle, there is a short window of time for this to occur. In like manner, we need to lay aside our doubts and fears and get into an intimate atmosphere with the Holy Spirit, with the Son of God, and with His Word. And as we do, then our spirit man becomes impregnated with His living and powerful *rhema* word. This will eventually result in giving birth to the needed tools, resources, ideas, creativity, and innovation, and the revelation of what we need to do in order to fulfill our God-given assignment on this earth.

Doubting Thomas clearly demonstrated to every born-again believer that we would have fearful or doubting moments, but we do not need to submit to them. And whenever we face those doubting moments, we then need to run to Jesus and grab ahold of Him, since it was Him who died on the cross and all of your fears, doubts, uncertainties, or insecurities were nailed there.

The challenge for you and I is to stop travelling on the road called "doubtful," to stop reading the "fear and doubt digest," to stop being around and listening to doubtful minds, and to move out of the house called "limitations." Remember, faith and the living Word of God is the antidote to fear and doubt.

Trusting the Lord with all your heart, mind, and strength is crucial to fulfilling your kingdom assignment on this earth.

Takeaway Lessons from the Life of Apostle Thomas

- Procrastination is full of hesitation and hesitation can delay you from boldly functioning in your calling.
- Fear and doubt are like two boxing gloves that are hitting you from the left and the right, which eventually sets your mental attitude with dizziness and confusion.
- Discovering and understanding your God-given identity will require faith. Walking and functioning in your kingdom purpose will also require faith. But fear and doubt will become your roadblock and will eventually detour you from the path you need to stay on.

41

THE IDENTITY OF THE WOMAN AT THE WELL

Nameless but Very Influential

T
he Bible is full of many extraordinary individuals that I have already outlined in this book, but there were two particular biblical characters that uniquely stand out from the rest of the crowd. The first one I have already outlined in Chapter twenty-nine, "The Identity of a Young Jewish Girl," and the second individual will be addressed in this chapter, "The Identity of the Woman at The Well."

There are a few unique factors about both of these individuals. Let us take a further look:

- Both were nameless
- Both were females
- One was a teenager, the other was a mature adult
- Both had major influence
- One was a slave because of captivity, the other was a slave because of her sinful lifestyle
- Both were referenced to water, where one water is symbolic to washing away our sins, while the other water is symbolic to satisfying our inner spirit man
- Both did extraordinary things

The fact that the Bible or the original writers did not include the names of these two unique individuals is remarkable and mysterious. I am glad that we have such extraordinary examples, both in the Old and in the New Testament. Also, I would like to stress another point in a firm way by addressing something that has been taking over our current culture like a virus and that is the whole notion that feminists are propagating, which is that women are treated as lower class. Some even boldly speak against the Bible by dictating that it is a book full of masculinity and female oppression.

Those who choose to believe this deception have not even cracked open a single page in the Bible. When we read through the Holy Scriptures, we see much emphasis that is placed on the role and the purpose of great women of

God, or those who exemplified remarkable deeds. And in this chapter, the story of the woman at the well once again gives greater credibility to the Word of God and to the fact that God is not an oppressor or someone who prefers one gender over the other.

Kingdom identity will never be restricted to a specific gender or to a specific skin color.

Nameless but Very Influential

Just as I have outlined valuable principles in chapter twenty-nine, I want to take this a step further by saying that God is not interested in your status, your fame, your financial well-being, your popularity, or your success in life. But God is very interested in your genuine heart, and in your willingness to submit to His purpose for your life.

In the Bible and throughout the history of Christianity, time and time again we witness God taking a nobody and making them into a somebody. Or we see where God takes a nameless person and makes them very influential. This is how God rolls! He does not follow a manmade rulebook or a list of qualifications! He is God and He does whatever He desires and however He desires!

The messed-up life of the woman at the well was transformed after just one encounter with the Savior! And this remarkable story once again underlines the truthful fact that all you need is a real encounter with Jesus and your whole life will be transformed. But it does not stop there! After having this encounter with Jesus, this same messed up woman ran to her city and began to evangelize to everyone. So, after you do have your personal encounter with the Savior, then your life, your mindset, your lifestyle, your perspective, and your purpose for living will become transformed. And then you will become an influential tool in God's hand that He will use to show others how great our God is.

Do not seek popularity, recognition, fame, or status, but seek the living water that Jesus is offering to you, so that His living waters can flow in you and through you. And a valuable life lesson that the woman at the well teaches us is that the living water only comes from Jesus. We also learn that only those who choose to come to Christ, who is the living water, will receive full internal satisfaction in their spirit man. Also, this profound story once again underlines the importance that no matter how messed up your life may be, just as long as you choose to come to Jesus and to humbly ask Him to fill your life and your spirit man with the living waters, then that will bring you true satisfaction in life.

In the Gospel of John, Jesus explained to the woman at the well that those who drink this earthly water will thirst again, but those who choose to drink the living water, that only Jesus gives, will never thirst again. This is a profound truth for all of God's children to grasp. And that truth is that none will ever be satisfied with the pleasures of this world and the only One who is able to give us true and eternal satisfaction is Christ Himself.

Only your divine identity will give you favor before others, not man's recognition.

Takeaway Lessons from the Life of the Woman at the Well

- Those who have discovered their God-given identity and purpose on earth will never seek men's applause or praises.
- As you discover for what purpose you were born, then it will become like a well of living water within you that will continually satisfy your spirit man.
- Your inner longing to fulfill your purpose can only be satisfied through Jesus and His Living Word.

42
THE IDENTITY OF THE PRODIGAL SON
You Are a Child of God

The story of the Prodigal Son is strongly evident in the lives of the younger generation, especially if they are still in Middle school, High school or in college. As I have mentioned before, I served as a youth pastor for many years and my heart is still focused on the younger generation, towards whom this whole book is primarily directed.

Often this powerful story is attributed to the scenario of us all being lost in this world and our heavenly Father waiting for us to come back home. This is true, but I want to take this opportunity to point out another perspective of this story where many from the younger generation feel like the Prodigal Son refers to Christianity and the Christian faith. I wrote a whole book entitled, *Generation Gap: Raising the Next Generation of Leaders* just addressing this whole issue, but in this chapter, I want to primarily focus on how our culture and society is creating "prodigal children" and how the body of Christ and the local church play an essential role in becoming the type of spiritual father who is able to re-connect these "prodigal children" back to their Creator, who is also their heavenly Father.

In this chapter, I will take another approach to the story of the Prodigal Son to help you understand that the younger generation is growing up in a prodigal society. And I will show why we need to focus and to direct the younger generation towards the heavenly Father who is the only One who can restore them and help them to discover their identity and to understand their kingdom assignment.

Humility is the fuel in your identity tank, while pride is the hole in it.

The Prodigal Society

The story of the Prodigal Son paints a portrait of our current society which has a prodigal mindset, a prodigal lifestyle, prodigal friendships and relationships, prodigal families, prodigal marriages, and a prodigal culture.

What does all of the above mean? The dictionary defines the word *prodigal* as: dissolute, extravagant, lavish, reckless, and wasteful.[1] The prodigal society and culture that has blossomed overnight like a mushroom has created the *I-want* and the *I-need* generation that is so desperately craving for excessive attention and for acceptance. And because of this, many live their daily life with a prodigal mindset.

One of the greatest challenges for all of us as we are surrounded with this type of prodigal society is to make sure that we never forsake the Father's house and do not get lured away with the appetites of this world. As we discover and understand more of who we are in Christ and who we need to become through Christ, then this prodigal society and culture will not appeal to our inner desires.

Here is a thought! Choose your friends in accordance with your purpose and destiny so that they will help you to arrive at your final destination. The prodigal culture and society heavily affect todays younger generation and it is no secret that your friendships or your associations do have an effect on your decision making, on your perception of life, and on how you view yourself. If the people that surround you live a life without purpose, then that will become your mindset also, or if most of your friends are struggling with their inner identity, then you likewise could struggle in this same area. But no matter how you may want to justify this, at the end of the day you are still fully responsible for your choices and what you desire for yourself, and for your future.

Do not go to your grave while you are still pregnant with dreams, vision, potential, and innovation. Know your purpose! And discover your purpose!

The Father Is Waiting for You

The parable of the Prodigal Son portrays one of the best illustrations of the heart of our heavenly Father towards His lost children! But the story is not limited to the reconciliation and the redemption of a lost soul. The Prodigal Son further exemplifies that when we eventually return to the arms of our Creator, who is also our heavenly Father, then we embark on the revelation and the reality of our divine identity.

When the Prodigal Son came to his senses, only then did he understand that the servants in his father's house were well fed, well taken care of, and were much better off than he was. This reality check that occurred in a pig pen speaks loud and clear into every heart and soul, that the world and the lust of this world will only lead you to a filthy pigpen while your heavenly Father is patiently waiting for you to come back to Him.

If you are tired of where you are in life, know that the Father is always waiting for you to come to Him! If you are lost and confused about your life's purpose, then likewise, the Father is waiting for you! And if you genuinely want to discover your purpose on this earth, then return to the Father just like the Prodigal Son did and He will place a ring of influence on your hand and give you a brand-new robe, representing your royalty status as a child of God. And when this occurs, you will no longer feel or be labeled as a Prodigal but will walk in your new identity as a child of God.

Your life is not a mere experiment since you were born on purpose to fulfil a specific purpose.

Takeaway Lessons from the Life of the Prodigal Son

- Your identity is hidden in the Father God. So, the more you abide in the Father the more you will know your God-given identity.
- Your identity and purpose will guide you to wisely choose your friends who will help you to reach your final destination.
- You first need to have a personal revelation that you are a child of God, which is your identity *in* Christ. And only then you will be able to discover and understand your identity *through* Christ, which is your kingdom assignment and purpose.

43

THE IDENTITY OF APOSTLE PAUL

What Type of Resume Do You Have?

The resume of Saul, before he became Apostle Paul was astounding. He was taught by one of the greatest religious leaders. He was multi-lingual. He was a Roman and a Hebrew citizen. He was a Pharisee. He was highly respected and feared amongst his peers.

You see, you can be very religious and not be relevant! You can be very spiritually minded but be so disconnected with people! You can recite most of the Bible, but have words proceeding out of your mouth that are saturated with divisiveness, hatred, envy, jealousy, and criticism! And one powerful observation that we can make from the life of Apostle Paul is that he went from being an extreme religious zealot to a loving individual who had a great servant's heart.

Yes, Apostle Paul is credited to have written most of the New Testament, but that was not because of how smart he was or because he had more favor of the Lord then the original disciples of Jesus, but because he grasped the revelation of who Jesus Christ was. And he was also willing to pay the price of servanthood and sacrifice so that he could become a needed and yielded vessel in the hands of God. And his life did exemplify this.

In this chapter, I will outline how someone can be so religious and spiritual but lack a true relationship with God. Also, you will discover how, often, others will get stuck on who you used to be and will have much difficulty accepting who the Lord has made you now. Additionally, you will understand why everyone needs to have their own Damascus Road encounter with Jesus. And finally, I will outline Apostle Paul's lengthy resume, which should challenge us all on how we need to be more sacrificial for our kingdom calling.

Those who know their kingdom identity become relational with God, but those who do not know their kingdom identity become more religious.

Full of Religiosity and Legalism, but Lacking the True Relationship

How is it possible to be so knowledgeable of the Scripture, so zealous for God, so disciplined in your spiritual life and yet again go directly against Jesus Himself? This was so true in the life of Saul. This was true throughout the history of Christianity; and this is even more true today in the lives of many Believers that are consistent church goers, Bible readers, and prayer warriors.

One of the key factors that left a sour taste in my heart and spirit when I was a teenager was when I would continually witness much religiosity in the lives of my fellow church goers and in the church leadership, but I did not see genuine relationships with Jesus resonating from them. This is no different in our current day Christianity, where many wear a religious mask, just like Saul did, and many are willing to persecute you, just because your theology, beliefs, or biblical revelations tend to differ from others.

Religiosity, man-made doctrines, theological ideology, and various dogmas in the body of Christ has created too many Sauls, and not enough Apostle Pauls. If you want to test this theory, then just go to YouTube and type in the words: Apostate Church, False Teachers, False Pastors, Church Deception, False Doctrine, and so on. You will be shockingly surprised how many thousands of videos you will find, and they will total more than one billion views and plenty of comments.

With that said, the spirit of legalism and religiosity has blinded and robbed the hearts of millions of Christians around the world. It is also the same spirit that has deprived many from understanding and discovering their true identity *in* Christ and their identity *through* Christ. Instead of these individuals being kingdom minded, they become spiritual judges, prosecutors, and executioners, just like Saul did as he would go from house to house arresting those who believed in Jesus.

Saul only did what he thought was best for him and for the religious order that was set by the Pharisees. This was totally the opposite of what Christ has called us to do. We are commissioned to serve our fellow man and not to demand others to submit to our own man-made ideologies or religiosity. God desires for His children to be relational, not religious. He wants them to be full of mercy and not judgmentalism and to have a servant's heart, not a heart full of legalism.

You will never successfully or authentically influence others until you discover your inner identity and purpose.

I Know Who You Are!

When I gave my life to the Lord during my senior year in High school, my life began to drastically change and transform. This is a divine process that every born-again believer goes through. With that said, I do remember a specific instance in my life that still resonates in my spirit man as a reminder of the supernatural power of God and the power of the blood of Jesus to truly transform someone's life and turn them one-hundred and eighty degrees in the right direction.

This situation occurred back in 2006 when I flew out to Seattle for training for a new job. When I was there, I remembered a couple who I wanted to visit since I knew the family well. When my parents chose to move to the state of Washington back in 1996, we actually lived with this family for about two months before my parents were able to find our own place. Anyway, during my stay in Seattle for my training, I reached out to this couple and asked if I could pay them a quick visit since it had been a while since I had seen them and I was also in the area.

The man said that he would call me back and let me know if things would align with our schedule, and eventually it did. When I came to their house that evening, the couples body language was a little strange and both of them had a kind of cautious look towards me. To make the long story short, towards the end of our fellowship, the atmosphere became more relaxed and we talked much about life and what I had been doing over the past years since we moved out of Washington.

The following morning when I was driving back to the airport, the man called me and thanked me again for visiting them while I was traveling for my job training. But something interesting occurred during this conversation. He said, "Stan I need to make a confession, and I need to apologize before you!" I was little perplexed thinking that I might have done something wrong, but he continued to explain the reason for his confession and apology by saying, "Stan, when you called me and told me that you were in the area and wanted to visit, my wife told me that she does not want this devil over to our house." I smirked with a little dismay, but he continued his confession, "You see Stan, years ago when your family moved here to Washington and lived in my house for about two months while your parents were looking for a house, your teenage behavior back then was treacherous and devil-like!" Again, these words made me a little uncomfortable, but the man continued, "So, I and my wife were very hesitant to have you over for dinner that evening but still decided to invite you."

What occurred further in this conversation was a personal testimony to me and a testimony to this particular couple. He concluded with these words, "Stan, having spent that evening with you and listening to all the great things that God has done in your life, and hearing that you were also a youth pastor and that God was using you in a powerful way to reach out to the younger generation truly blessed me and my wife."

What additionally occurred that evening and in the process was a sign and a confirmation of the almighty power of the Holy Spirit and the power of the blood of Jesus that can transform the heart and mind of an individual. My life became a living testimony to that couple who remembered me as a little mischievous and devilish teenager, but that evening they saw a whole new Stan!

Just like this occurred in my life, this also occurs in every born-again person as they go through a similar transformation process. One of the greatest witnesses that we all carry is when we encounter people from our previous life or those who use to know us as filthy sinners are now seeing us as holy and righteous saints.

My personal testimony is not limited to me only, and as we observe the transformation of Saul into Apostle Paul, we also learn that he went through his own period of opposition by other Believers. Back then, Christian Jews saw the killer Saul, but God saw Apostle Paul and a writer of most of the New Testament. Why? Before his Damascus Road encounter, the Believers heard of killer Saul who was persecuting Christians, but now he was a transformed individual and a devout follower of Christ.

Apostle Paul's transformation was magnificent, but it took some time for even the disciples of Jesus to believe that he was transformed, and that Jesus gave him a powerful assignment to fulfill. The transformational power of the Holy Spirit through the blood of Jesus is truly a phenomenon that cannot always be explained through words but needs to be witnessed by others.

"I know who you are!" is a phrase that should become a witnessing opportunity to show others how God can change and transform someone like me, who God took from being branded as a little devil to becoming a youth pastor. Or to show the transformation of someone like the killer, Saul, who discovered his purpose and is accredited to have written most of the New Testament.

Knowing your purpose will make you into an agent of change.

Everyone Needs to Have Their Own Damascus Road Encounter

The most transformational moment in the life of Apostle Paul occurred on the Damascus Road as he was full of religious zeal to hunt down Believers and followers of Jesus. When Jesus spoke to him through a bright light, He asked Saul a profound question, "Saul, Saul, why are you persecuting Me?"[1] This question was referring to why Saul was going against the will of God. And it is at this very important moment where Saul did something amazing, which every living human being needs to do in their life. Saul asked Jesus a follow up question: "Who are You, Lord?"[2]

It would be fair to say that Saul was zealous for God and earnestly desired to please God through his life, and he sincerely thought that as he would persecute and arrest the followers of Jesus, that would be please God. This was so because Saul believed that the followers of Jesus were heretics and were spreading a false doctrine. But when he had his personal encounter with Jesus, Saul understood that it was God who was talking with him and did not begin to question the credibility of this audible voice. He only wanted clarity, and the clarity that he received was again through an audible voice saying, "I am Jesus, whom you are persecuting."[3] In like manner, every living human being will have their own type of encounter with the Truth, which is Jesus, and when they do, they will understand that they have been going against the will of God for their own personal life.

As much as this is so important, Jesus says something very interesting to Saul, "It is hard for you to kick against the goads."[4] What does that mean? A *goad* is a stick with a pointed or electrically charged end, for driving cattle or oxen, and the more that the animal will resist, the more pain it will bring upon itself. This is also true that the more we resist or go against the will of God for our life, the more pain, frustration, fear, doubt, and uncertainty we create in our personal life.

What also made the Damascus Road encounter truly unique, was that Saul did not go into a back and forth argumentative dialogue with Jesus, but just asked Him a simple question: "Lord, what do You want me to do?"[5] This is the exact same thing every born-again believer needs to ask for their personal life and for their personal purpose on this earth.

When we have our own personal Damascus Road encounter with Jesus, then we will be able to truly understand our purpose, our existence, and what Jesus desires for us to do in our life and through our life. Until then, we may be faithful church goers, stable in our prayer life, and disciplined in reading the

Word of God, but until we have our personal encounter with Jesus, we could end up like a religious zealot, just like Saul was.

Anointing in combination with your kingdom purpose will make you into an influential ambassador of Christ.

Apostle Paul's Resume

It is hard for anyone to grasp the biblical insight as it relates to us facing much opposition, various persecutions, betrayal, hatred, being despised, receiving verbal or physical attacks and sometimes even being martyred for the sake of the Lord or His Truth. The Bible is full of references to these things because the children of the devil hate the children of God.

Every biblical character has a specific resume and Apostle Paul's resume distinctively stands out from others. Let us take a look at some of these distinctive qualifications from Paul's career:

- Whipped five times with thirty-nine stripes[6]
- Three times beaten with rods[7]
- Once stoned and left for dead[8]
- Three times involved in shipwrecks[9]
- Experienced numerous and various perils[10]
- Often experienced sleeplessness, hunger, thirst, and fasting[11]

Apostle Paul's resume is truly remarkable and we as Believers take much pride and joy in his achievements, but seldom do we look at our own personal resume. Yes, we all have our own resume that we write up as we live on this earth. I guess the big question would be, what will others read on our resume once we have departed from this earth? The identity of Apostle Paul is powerful and his resume is mesmerizing, but we who are still alive on this earth need to seriously take a look at our own resume which is only a reflection of our God-given identity and the assignment that we need to fulfill on this earth while we still can. And I conclude this chapter with these powerful words from Apostle Paul, "I, therefore, the prisoner of the Lord, beseech you to walk worthy of the calling with which you were called, with all lowliness and gentleness, with longsuffering, bearing with one another in love, endeavoring to keep the unity of the Spirit in the bond of peace."[12]

As you begin to walk and function in your kingdom purpose, God then begins to build your spiritual resume.

Takeaway Lessons from the Life of Apostle Paul

- Do not go to the grave still full of your kingdom potential but live in such a way that others will still talk about you and what you did, even after you are gone.
- While some will try to remind you of who you use to be, you need to continually stay focused on who the Lord has made you now.
- Religiosity and legalism are signs that someone does not know their God-given identity and purpose.

44
THE IDENTITY OF JUDAS ISCARIOT
Existing but Not Living

One of the greatest tragedies about Judas Iscariot is not necessarily how his life ended but that he walked side by side with the Son of God for more than three years and still did not discover his God-given identity and purpose. And as much as that may be tragic, there is something that is likewise tragic amongst so many Christians Believers who have been going to church and have been reading the Bible for years and still have not discovered their God-given identity and purpose.

In my early years as a believer, I struggled many times with my inner identity and purpose as there were no genuine or credible spiritual mentors who guided me through my personal growth process. As a result, my perception of church, God, and the Bible were a little distorted, and over time, I became discouraged. This is the same issue that so many Christians Believers around the world experience, resulting in that they simply do not discover and understand their purpose on this earth, their existence, and what their kingdom assignment is.

This also results in many individuals leaving the church and falling away from God, not always necessarily due to sinful behaviors or lifestyles but because they were not able to discover their God-given identity and purpose. And in this chapter, I will share a couple of insightful aspects in reference to Judas Iscariot that reflect on many individuals today. First, you will understand why many people are simply existing on earth, but not living. And secondly, you will get clarity on why many have allowed demonic or religious deception to take ahold of their mind and heart, thinking that God has already predestined some things to happen in our life which we cannot change which totally contradicts our ability to exercise our free will.

Until you discover your purpose for life, you will just simply be existing on this earth.

Existing but Not Living

When you honestly evaluate your life, ask yourself this serious question, "Am I living or am I existing?" Many people just go through life, but never live through their life. And in the tragic story of Judas Iscariot, he walked side-by-side with the life giver but was not able to enjoy that life because he closed himself off in his own box of selfishness, self-centeredness, and greed.

This leads me to point out another important factor that we have too many Christians Believers who regularly attend church, or who regularly read God's Word, or who even regularly pray, but in their life, they are experiencing a spiritual identity crisis and feel like they are simply existing and not living. For as long as the light switch is in the off mode, the light will never shine. For as long as the new car is sitting idle in the garage day after day, then the car will never fulfill its original purpose. And for as long as any living human being is not living out or walking in their God-given identity and purpose, then that person is simply existing.

When we carefully evaluate the life of Judas Iscariot, we can get legalistically distracted by his greedy heart and by his betrayal of Jesus for a lousy thirty pieces of silver. But Judas' short outlined life in the Bible and his encounter with Jesus still shines much knowledge and insight that absolutely every born-again believer can grasp as a crucial revelation for their personal life.

Judas was not the most horrible or evil person, but just an individual who exemplified the true reality of someone who can go to church, who can read the Bible, who can pray, or who can sincerely believe in Jesus, but still have a severe case of spiritual identity crisis. This was not limited to Judas and Peter alone but is very much evident in absolutely every local church. Remember, the thief comes to steal, kill, and destroy!

When I served as a youth pastor and as an ordained minister in my first church, I personally came across my own spiritual identity crisis. As the Lord helped me through it, my heart and spirit man was hungry for more and I was willing to pay the price. I have observed, and still observe many Christians struggling mainly in this area of their life. To be honest, my personal observation and interactions with many has allowed me to come to the conclusion that it is not necessarily the sin that is devastating many Christians or why many leave their local church, but it is actually that many are struggling to understand their identity *in* Christ and their identity *through* Christ.

Judas' life ended with a tragic suicide, which happens to be a growing trend that we are painfully witnessing in today's society. The fact that Judas took his own life should provide the importance of this matter for us because many who lose hope and purpose in life tragically end their life in suicide.

Why? Because as soon as a person comes to the realization that they are simply existing in this world, then they tend to lose focus and meaning for their true purpose and existence on this earth. Once that individual has cornered them self, with the assistance of the deceiver, then they begin to convince themselves that there is no reason for them to continue to simply exist on earth and they tragically end their own life.

We could argue that Judas painfully struggled with the fact that he betrayed the Son of God, which is true, but we cannot ignore the importance that for more than three years, he walked side-by-side with Jesus and witnessed some of the greatest miracles that most Christians will never experience or witness in their whole life. Judas' greatest struggle was not his greed for money or his hate for Jesus, but the struggle of trying to discover who he was and what purpose and potential was still lying dormant inside of him. Yes, it is more than possible for you to exist in life, but never live that life that God has already predestined for you. Additionally, the world and our society is saturated with individuals who are simply existing and not living, but that does not need to be so, and for this main reason, Jesus came into the world to once and for all reconnect, reconcile, and to re-activate in all of us our original God-given identity, so that we could live life in its fulness.

> **God has already predestined your future and your purpose on this earth. All you have to do is just submit to His perfect will for your life.**

Was Judas' Fate Already Predestined?

In my early years as a believer, I heard plenty of interesting and contradicting things from my fellow Believers and from preachers, and one of them was that Judas' fate was already predestined or predetermined by God! If that is the case, then where does our *free will* come into play? Or what about the daily choices that we make? Or what about the law of sowing and reaping?

Those who choose to believe such a legalistic and even dangerous theology are blindly robing and binding themselves with doctrinal handcuffs. Judas Iscariot had the opportunity to repent from his sins every day or to personally reach out to Jesus and ask for His guidance as it related to his purpose and to his existence. And I highly doubt that Jesus would say, "Well Judas, I am glad that you asked! But, to be honest with you, my Father has already predestined you to betray me so that I would be crucified on the cross. So, sorry, I cannot help you!"

Again, ask yourself this honest non-theological question, does God really choose or appoint specific individuals throughout humanity like Hitler, or Stalin, or Saddam Hussein, or the school mass shooters who would carry out such atrocities in our world? Of course not! But we do hear this nonsense plenty of times on news networks, "Why would the almighty lovable God allow this tragedy to happen?" Sorry, but that is a stupid question to pose in the first place!

Judas' fate was not predestined! Judas did not get the short end of the stick! And Judas was not the chosen scapegoat that God had appointed since the foundation of this world. The truth is, that God already knew what choice Judas would make and because of this he eventually walked out and even fulfilled what was prophesied in the Old Testament.

Why do we have laws? Why do we have specific rules and regulations? And why do parents restrict or discipline their child in certain ways? All of the above is meant to protect the individual, but as soon as anyone breaks or violates a law, a rule, or a family order, there will be consequences. The law will not punish you unless you break it. And no normal parent will discipline their child when they have done nothing wrong. In the same manner, God has already laid out His blueprint through the Word of God which teaches many things that pertain to life, salvation, eternity, blessings, miracles, and to punishment.

Our heavenly Father does not desire that anyone should perish or burn in the lake of fire for eternity and He also does not desire for any of His children to suffer or struggle in unnecessary pain or turmoil on this earth. With that said, yes, we will go through many challenges, trials, and stormy weather, but God promised us that He will never leave us nor forsake us. So, we do have hope! We do have something to look forward to! We can trust in God's promises that are saturated in the pages of our Bible.

God wants you to live a life of purpose and not to simply exist on this earth. God desires for every living human being to know Him and to know their inner identity. And God is not an angry old man who is eagerly looking forward to smiting someone dead, just because they did something wrong or something sinful! So remember, you have not been predestined by God to walk in a similar path as Judas Iscariot who would live a purposeless life on this earth. But you were called, you were appointed, you were chosen and ordained before the foundations of this world to do something awesome and purposeful!

When you die, if you are only remembered and missed by your family and friends, then you did not live a life of purpose.

172

Takeaway Lessons from the Life of Judas Iscariot

- Your identity was already predestined by God, but it is up to you to discover it.
- Many are simply existing in the world and not living because they have not discovered their God-given identity and purpose.
- Whenever you do not understand your identity, potential, gifts, or talents, you will automatically begin to abuse them or use them for the wrong purpose.

45
THE IDENTITY OF LUCIFER
The Founder and the CEO of Identity Theft

The identity of Lucifer very much differs in comparison to the rest of the biblical characters that I have outlined in this book. But why did I choose to include him in a form of identity?

What is so unique about the identity of Lucifer is that he is desperately trying to make his dark and eternally condemned identity part of the identity of every living human being, which is very similar the goal of Christ who is eagerly interested in helping each individual to discover their Christ-like identity. And these two identities will continually be at war with each other.

When I was first introduced to chapter twenty-eight in the book of Ezekiel and to chapter fourteen in the book of Isaiah through one of my spiritual mentors, I was truly surprised to discover in detail who Lucifer was. Let us look at a quick outline of who this majestic cherub was before his fall:

- *Son of the morning*
- *Seal of perfection*
- *Full of wisdom*
- *Perfect in beauty*
- *He was anointed*
- *He was established*
- *Was on the holy Mountain of God*
- *Walked in the midst of fiery stones*
- *He was perfect in his ways when he was created*
- *Covered in precious stones (diamond, gold, emerald, sapphire, jasper, onyx, topaz)*

Now that is a solid resume to have! I guess the big question is, how did such a glorious and a majestic cherub get fired from heaven and expelled from the presence of God? Let us take a deeper look at the detailed list which the book of Ezekiel in chapter twenty-eight provides for us:

- Iniquity was found in him
- Became filled with violence
- His heart was lifted up because of his beauty

- His wisdom became corrupted because of his splendor
- He said in his heart: *"I will ascend into heaven, I will exalt my throne above the stars of God; I will also sit on the mount of the congregation. I will be like the Most High."*[1]

As much as Lucifer's original resume looked very prestige, the list of reasons why he was fired by God was a greater depiction of who he was. And in this chapter, I will outline some thought-provoking insight on how powerful the spirit of Lucifer is, why he is the masterful identity thief, and finally, how the identity of Lucifer is crippling many Christians and destroying many church leaders.

The day you discover and understand your kingdom identity and purpose will be the day you will be assigned demonic agents who will do whatever they can to distract, to divert, and to detour you from fulfilling your purpose on this earth.

The Spirit of Lucifer

I have come to the realization that the number one tactic that Lucifer uses to get born-again Believers out of their God-given purpose and assignment is not necessarily sin, but taking God's original Word and using it against them by twisting the true essence of what God has already said. This was very evident when Satan tempted Jesus three times in the wilderness by using the Word to challenge Jesus.

The spirit of Lucifer and its functionality is usually evident in these seven primary areas:

1. Division
2. Rebellion
3. Witchcraft (Control and Manipulation)
4. The Lust for Power (Position and Status)
5. Challenging God's Authority (The Bible)
6. Challenging Leadership Authority in the Body of Christ

7. Speaking Evil of Your Fellow Brother or Sister in the Lord (Criticism, Gossip, or Open Rebuke)

Some of you reading the following may not agree with my insight, but allow me to pose a few thought provoking questions:

- It has been estimated that the Protestant sphere has more than 40,000 denominations. Are all these denominations because of sin or because of manmade interpretation of Scriptures?
- Are most church splits, divisions, and tensions because of sin or because the leadership could not agree with certain theological or doctrinal beliefs?
- Is tension and frustration between church leaders because of them living a sinful lifestyle or because they cannot come into agreement with certain biblical truths?
- And why do Baptists resist the Pentecostals belief as it relates to the baptism of the Holy Spirit? Or why do conservatives mock the Charismatics? Or why do many prominent denominations criticize the Catholics for the emphasis placed on the mother Mary instead of Jesus?

All the above has nothing to do with sin but everything to do with each denomination interpreting the Word of God in ways that fit best with their spiritual comfort zone.

That was definitely a mouth full! You see, the spirit of Lucifer takes the truth and twists it to make it fit into the comfortability of each individual and then when these two individuals get together, they begin to argue, debate and even rebuke one another. For example, Jesus did so many supernatural miracles, but the religious pastors of His day mocked Him, because He did it on the Sabbath day. The disciples of Jesus were opposed to Apostle Paul preaching the gospel to the Gentiles and some even forced the Gentiles to be circumcised in accordance with the Mosaic Law.

To this day, the Bible is still considered as one of the most controversial and contentious books in all of history. Endless arguments, debates, and fighting have and continue to occur between Believers and unBelievers over the content of the Scriptures.

When I was in youth ministry, most of my heated arguments and debates between church leaders and fellow Believers were not over sin or sinful lifestyles, but over the interpretation and the true meaning of Scriptures. Today, I and my family are privileged to be members of Free Chapel and to be under the spiritual leadership of Pastor Jentezen Franklin where our church has global impact and influence. But with that said, I still come across some of our church folks and other Believers who complain about our theology, or that the music is too loud, or because we have smoke machines, or that we are too Charismatic, and the religious list just goes on and on.

You see, for the longest time I use to have a very narrow-minded view when it came to church divisions, splits, tensions amongst leaders, the pointing of fingers at a fellow brother or sister in the Lord, or the hatred through the social media. My understanding was that it was the devil's fault and the devil was using the Believers against one another. And I was convinced that these Believers were being influenced by demonic spirits. There is some truth to this, but over the years I have come to a whole different understanding.

One of the primary reasons for all of the above chaos and divisiveness in the body of Christ is due to the fact that most of those Believers who get caught up in contentions, divisions, envy, or other nonsense is because they do not know their God-given identity and are facing a spiritual identity crisis. This is as plain and simple as I can state it. I do not just say this blatantly, but it is something that I have observed and continue to observe in the body of Christ, and something that I have also personally experienced in my early years as a Christian.

There was a season when I would indulge myself with YouTube videos entitled, False Teachers and Prophets, The Apostate Church, Christian Deception, Pastors of Deception, and the list would go on and on. The issue that arose in the process of this search was that most of these Christian ministers or ministries were negatively talking about other fellow Christians. And those ministers whom they negatively spoke about, I personally enjoyed listening to and watching. At one point, I was confused and then eventually stopped watching or listening to any content that fell into this subject matter.

I do remember one instance where I wrote a comment under one particular YouTube video that dedicated two radio talk shows that were about two hours long, to mainly focus on exposing and talking ill about one particular minister whom I had great respect for, so I decided to make a comment. I wrote, "Why are you wasting your time and your potential on speaking ill against this man of God? Focus your gift and platform on building the kingdom of God." His response was, "I'm using my gift and building the kingdom of God by exposing this false teacher." And, my follow up response was, "Since when did the Bible include a spiritual gift that was called The Gift of a Spiritual Police Officer?"

Eventually I did not want to continue this dialogue, but sadly enough this video already had thousands of views and by now it is probably in the millions. Anyway, the danger here is that this particular believer had an inner conviction to utilize his gift and platform to expose this particular minister.

With that said, I do want to pose the thought that some important individual once said, "Every kingdom divided against itself is brought to desolation, and every city or house divided against itself will not stand."[2] Does this sound familiar? Oh yeah, Jesus said this!

It honestly does not matter what convictions you may have or how you may justify your ministry calling and assignment, anyone who speaks ill of their fellow brother or sister in the Lord is fulfilling the words of the above Scripture. This is why the body of Christ has so many divisions and splits and so much envy and hatred, and too many of these people are actually going against God's will and also contradict the Scripture by trying to justify their holy and righteous behaviors, just like this person was doing through their YouTube channel. This is where the enemy has infiltrated the body of Christ convincing many Believers that they are doing the Lord's work. But this is the work of the spirit of Lucifer and this is also a major sign of those who do not know their identity in Christ and their identity through Christ.

Pride, egoism, jealousy, and the lust for power are the ingredients for an identity crisis.

The Founder and CEO of Identity Theft

Without argument, Lucifer is the founder and CEO of identity theft! And Jesus confirmed this by saying, "The thief does not come except to steal, and to kill, and to destroy."[3] Lucifer is also called the father of lies,[4] and it is through his lies and deceptions that he successfully robs many born-again Believers from their faith, from their purpose, from their calling, from their blessing, and from their God-given identity. And one of the most successful tactics of the devil is to continually remind you of your past, of who you were, and what immoral or sinful deeds that you have done. And as soon as he is able to grab ahold of your heart, your mind, your spirit man, and even your emotions with this deception, he then begins to draw a glooming future for you with thoughts such as: "You are a defect!" Or, "You will never be happy or successful." Or, "You are a loser who will not be able to achieve anything in life!"

In other words, if we allow the devil to pull us back into our past, then he will become successful in robbing our future which will result in us aborting our purpose and assignment on this earth. Identity theft is a growing crisis and often it deals with monetary issues, but most of the victims usually recover and move on. But spiritual identity theft is an internal issue that many have not recovered from and their lives were snuffed out. They also became full of anger, bitterness, despair, hopelessness, and much anger at God. And the only way to recover from such spiritual identity theft is to wholeheartedly run into the hands of our heavenly Father and with humility and repentance ask Him to restore what the enemy has stolen from us.

Lucifer is the father of lies and a professional agent of deception. Since he is not limited by earthly time, he will craftily work his way to your heart and into your mind as he slowly begins to rob you of your faith, your time, your kingdom assignment and purpose, your health, and eventually rob you of your existence on this earth. But there is always hope for us since we also have a secret undercover agent, the Holy Spirit, who is able to uncover and expose every demonic trickery that Lucifer has up his sleeves. And no matter what he deceptively tries to do against us, we can always count on the words of the Apostle John, "You are of God, little children, because He who is in you is greater than he who is in the world."[5]

No matter how deceptive, destructive, or devastating the identity of Lucifer may be, there is great news! We all know the future destiny of this age-old serpent and that is the lake of fire where he will burn for eternity and will never be able to oppose or to harass God's children ever again.

If you despise or disregard your kingdom identity, then do not be surprised if Satan, the masterful thief, ends up robbing you of your purpose on this earth.

Takeaway Lessons from the Life of Lucifer

- Numerous individuals continue to have their identities stripped away from them because of sinful lifestyles or because they dishonor the gift that was within them.
- The devil does not need to kill you or bring physical harm to your body. All he needs to do is to rob you of your kingdom identity, and by doing so, he has made you into a defect where you are no longer an asset but a liability on earth.
- Divisiveness, manipulation, witchcraft, hatred, rebellion, and the lust for power are all symptoms of the spirit of Lucifer.

46
THE IDENTITY OF JESUS
The Way, the Truth, and the Life

As I bring you towards the last and the final biblical character, I do have to finalize everything by saying that Jesus is the only qualified being that is authorized to help you discover your identity *in* Christ and then your identity *through* Christ. He is also the only One that can confirm in you the original proclamation that was spoken by God in Genesis, "Then God said, 'Let Us make man in Our image, according to Our likeness.'"[1]

In this particular chapter you will discover the humanity of Jesus and His divine kingdom assignment on this earth. You will also learn how much Jesus was able to accomplish in less than four years of His purpose on earth. Also, you will know why it is so vital to have your identity to always abide in Him. I will also address that death is the graduation from your earthly kingdom assignment. And finally, I will talk about a sobering question, Who do people say that you are?

Only those who have discovered their God-given identity will be able to walk in the Spirit and be able to resist the lust of the flesh.

Jesus Was No Exception

We should never be ignorant to the fact that Jesus was both the Son of God and the Son of Man, and because He was the Son of Man, He was not exempt to the attacks and the temptations of the devil. When Jesus was fasting and in the wilderness for forty days and forty nights, the devil tempted Him and each of his temptations was solely focused on the identity of Jesus. The following are these three strategic attacks on Jesus' identity:

1. "If you are the Son of God, command that these stones become bread."[2]
2. "If you are the Son of God, throw Yourself down."[3]

3. "All these things I will give You if You will fall down and worship me."[4]

These attacks were not only coming from Satan but also from the local people who knew Jesus. Here is the classic illustration of this:

When He had come to His own country, He taught them in their synagogue, so that they were astonished and said, "Where did this Man get this wisdom and these mighty works? Is this not the carpenter's son? Is not His mother called Mary? And His brothers James, Joses, Simon, and Judas?"[5]

And Jesus adds to this when He speaks in the following passages:

Then He said, "Assuredly, I say to you, no prophet is accepted in his own country."[6]

But Jesus said to them, "A prophet is not without honor except in his own country, among his own relatives, and in his own house."[7]

Those who choose to ignore the above passages and be ignorant to the fact that as much as God uses people to help us to discover and to fulfill our purpose on earth, in like manner the devil will use people to discourage, divert, criticize, mock, and oppose our God-given identity and purpose. Jesus was not exempt from being opposed or called a blasphemous heretic. Why? Because He knew His kingdom identity and assignment and that intimidated others, especially the religious leaders. And this should also be an encouragement to all of us, since we are no greater than He is.

When you fully and totally surrender your life to God, He will begin to do impossible things in and through your God-given calling and purpose.

Is That Even Possible?

The more we read about the life, the purpose, and the deeds of Jesus, the more we become encouraged, surprised, and awed by who He was and the hope that

He gave to all humanity. But here I want to point out something very specific as it solely relates to our subject matter. Who Jesus was and what He did is extremely remarkable but let us not forget how much He accomplished in just about three and a half years!

Is that even possible? Well, for Jesus it was! But could that same principle apply for you and I? Absolutely, yes! We usually limit ourselves or even bind ourselves to a specific timeframe or to a specific season in our lives. For example, it took Noah more than 100 years to build the ark, but his official assignment was completed in less than 400 days once the water fully receded. Moses' assignment did not start until he was around eighty years old. Abraham and Sarah discovered their identity and purpose in their retirement years.

In other words, each and every individual's assignment and purpose are different and will not have the same timeline or timeframe or time cycle. In my specific case, in my early twenties, I was a youth pastor for about ten years. After that, for about five years, it seemed that nothing was happening in my life at all. As a matter of fact, it was during those five years that I faced some of my most challenging moments. I was so confused with what God was doing during that season of my life that I remember one particular situation where I began to hate the previous season of my youth ministry, thinking that it was a waste of my personal time.

At that moment, I knew that I was going through my spiritual identity crisis and by God's superabundant grace He helped me to go through that devastating season. My main point here is that I was going through a transitional season in my life, but to me it seemed to be going so slow, like a snail trying to sprint. The lesson here is that every individual will face different seasons in their life. Some will be active early on in their lives, while others will be fully active later in their lives, and others will go through stages and phases in their lives. But no matter how your purpose and assignment on this earth has been written by our heavenly Father, we should never lose focus. Remember that He is in control and we just need to fully trust and surrender ourselves into His hands! And yes, God will make it possible!

God did not command you to look for your kingdom identity, but to discover it through Jesus Christ.

Your Identity Will Go Through Various Stages

God does not live in time nor is He limited by time like we are! With that said, we often look back on our past with much regret; we observe our present with certain confusion and uncertainties, and we ponder about our futures with fear and doubt. The Word of God declares, "Jesus Christ is the same yesterday, today, and forever."[8]

When it comes to our identity, it can be analyzed in three stages. Allow me to elaborate:

1. *The Past Stage:* Who we were in the past as sinners without Christ does not define who God created us to be, but the devil has crafty ways to try to remind and to draw us back into our previous life or lifestyle.
2. *The Present Stage:* It is this phase of our life that is crucial as we begin our journey in discovering our God-given purpose and assignment.
3. *The Future Stage:* Even though the future is not fully revealed or even understood by many born-again Believers, we need to eagerly look forward with faith to what has already been predestined for us to fulfill and to accomplish through our purpose and calling on this earth.

Whatever stage of your life you may be in right now, always know that time will never be your friend, so become a close friend with Jesus because He is not limited or restricted by time. He will help you to go through all of the stages of your life.

As soon as you disconnect yourself from God, the Original source, your identity will begin to fade away and you will automatically begin to detour from your kingdom purpose.

Your Identity Should Always Abide in Him

The gospel of John outlines a powerful passage where Jesus refers to Himself as the true vine and to us as the branches: "I am the vine, and you are the branches. He who abides in Me, and I in him, bears much fruit; for without Me you can do nothing."[9]

Just as any branch that is cut away or separated from the original source ends up withering and dying, in like manner, will this happen to everyone who thinks that they can live apart from Jesus or try to walk in their destiny without Jesus. Jesus also sternly says, that without Him we can never bear any fruit. In other words, our identity and purpose will become void and useless if we decide to go solo, thinking that we have the ability or the knowledge or the tools to live a life of independence from God. Many Believers have become like withered branches, and as a result, their hearts have been stirred up with anger, hatred, and bitterness towards God. But they did not know that they did not choose to remain in Him, and this resulted in their life being fruitless.

Your God-given identity needs to always abide in Him. If you choose to disconnect from Him then it will only be a matter of time until your faith and His Word begin to diminish, just like any Smartphone that continually needs to be recharged if you desire to use it for beneficial purposes. Whenever your faith goes dry, then your connection to your heavenly Father gets interrupted, which could result in much devastation that you allowed into your life. Always stay connected to the true source by remaining in Him.

Knowing your kingdom identity and purpose will discipline you in carrying your cross daily.

Death Is Only the Finish Line

Death or dying is never a comfortable thing to think about and it is not the most exciting conversation topic to discuss with others. With that said, the Scriptures are full of encouraging words as it relates to death.

We often hear preachers and other fellow Believers say that we need to walk in the footsteps of Jesus. And as I wrap up this chapter, I would like to challenge every reader with this same notion by offering the following thought-provoking questions and statements:

- Two things usually make an individual very influential and very dangerous: first, when they have discovered their purpose and existence on earth, and second, when they are willing to die for what they believe in.

- When you die, will you be remembered beyond your cemetery stone or will your purpose and potential become buried with you?
- Do not allow your future grave to rob this world of the hidden potential that abides within you.

The book of Romans declares that we were baptized and united into His death, and we will also be in likeness of His resurrection, as Christ died and resurrected, so shall we also die in Christ and be resurrected into His eternal glory.[10] So death is not the end, but only the finish line for those Believers who have died in Christ.

Just like the mirror, God is the only credible source that can truly reveal who you are, why you were born, and what your purpose is on this earth.

Jesus' Mother and Siblings Doubted Him

Jesus' mother and siblings doubted Him. Are you serious? How could they doubt the Son of God? Let us take a look at two passages that reveal this to be the truth:

While Jesus was still talking to the people, His mother and His brothers came and stood outside. They wanted to talk to Him. Someone said to Him, "Your mother and brothers are outside and want to talk to you."[11]

The brothers of Jesus said to Him, "Leave here and go to the country of Judea. Let Your followers there see the things You do. If a person wants others to know what he is doing, he does things to be seen. Since You are doing such things, show Yourself to the world." Not even His brothers were putting their trust in Him.[12]

The hardcore truth is that often spouses, family members, and siblings will not always grasp or understand the engraved, God-given identity and kingdom calling that their family member or loved one possesses and they could even resist it. If Jesus experienced this with His mother and with His siblings, then you and I are no exception.

Jesus is the only authorized individual that can activate, define, and reveal your kingdom identity. Everyone else around you is only authorized to confirm your kingdom identity.

Who Do People Say That (Stan Belyshev) Is?

I purposely inserted my name in the above parenthesis, but as you read this section, insert your name instead. In the example of this section, I will pose the question again but with my name: *Who do people say that Stan Belyshev is?* As you read through this last section of this chapter, allow this powerful question to resonate in your heart, in your mind, and in your spirit man. Why? Because this is the same question Jesus asked His disciples when He said, "Who do people say that the Son of Man is?"[13]

This question is the universal identity question! If you pose this question to the devil about yourself, then he will have his own answer for you. If you go to your family members or your friends, then they will have their own answer for you. If you turn to the social media or to the entertainment industry, then likewise they will also have their own specific answer for you. And even if you ask your parents, in their limited understanding, they will do their best to answer this question for you but may still miss the mark. Only when you come to Jesus will you be able to truly learn and discover who you are and for what purpose you were created on this earth.

Consider the purpose of the items in the following statements, to help you to get more clarity about your kingdom purpose:

- *Keys unlock doors and locks!*
- *Gasoline makes a car run!*
- *Lightbulbs give light!*
- *Cows produce milk!*
- *Batteries enable products to function in their originally designed purpose!*

I guess the question you and I need to ask is, what were you and I born to do and to fulfill on this earth?

My challenge to you and I is to always go to the original source, to the author and the finisher of your life. Only He is able to tell you the real truth of who you are, whose you are, why you were born, and what purpose you were created to fulfill on this earth. Discover your identity *in* Christ and your identity *through* Christ today by receiving into your heart and spirit man the identity of Jesus!

Know the Word, live by the Word, and release the Word, and by doing so, you will fulfill your kingdom purpose.

Takeaway Lessons from the Life of Jesus

- As you discover Jesus, who is the Way, the Truth, and the Life, in the process, you will discover the path for your life. And you will also receive much knowledge and wisdom through the person of Jesus as it relates to your purpose.
- God will never be limited or restricted by time or by life circumstances. And as long as you and I are walking with Jesus, then nothing and no one will hinder us from fulfilling our kingdom assignment.
- We should never fear or be intimidated by death. Why? Because death is a sign that our kingdom assignment on this earth has come to its completion.

PART 3

Protect Your Identity! Fight for Your Purpose! Fulfill Your Kingdom Assignment on This Earth!

47
THE AGE-OLD THIEF

Just as God's original desire and intention for your identity and purpose has not changed, in like manner, *the age-old thief* from the Garden of Eden has also not changed his original desire, and that is the desire to strip you of your God-given identity and purpose. And Apostle Peter sternly warns us about this age-old thief: "The thief does not come except to steal, and to kill, and to destroy."[1]

When the Scriptures refer to the devil as a *thief*, this is not meant to be a cute statement, but a cautionary declaration for all Believers to seriously ponder. What is typically the purpose or the function of any thief? They unlawfully take what is not originally theirs. In other words, the thief did not invest their time, their finances, or their sweat and blood into whatever they are stealing. This illustrates the magnificent portrait of the ultimate price that Jesus paid for us all on the cross as He hung there, drenched in His own blood, and eventually died. Last time I checked, I do not remember the devil dying for anyone!

So why is the devil considered "the age-old thief"? Because of his hatred and jealousy towards God and towards all of God's creation! You see, the originality and the uniqueness of your fingerprints only confirm how you are individually unique within your family, community, society, and so on. But this thief wants to steal your God-given identity, so you can become just as miserable and hopeless as he is.

Do Not Lay Your Responsibility upon the Shoulders of God

Just as any relationship or friendship is a two-way street, in a similar manner God fulfills His role, and we need to fulfill our role. God has already predestined everything for us and all we need to do is discover our identity, purpose, and assignment on earth and then, with God's help and assistance, walk it out and fulfill it. One common and flawed mistake that many Believers make is to sit idle and wait until God starts to do something.

Our God is a God of action and He will not move in us or through us unless we give Him full permission to do so. This thought usually baffles many Christians since it looks like we need to give God permission to use us as a vessel for His purpose. Well, yeah! On the flip side though, the age-old thief, the devil, will prompt you with supposedly wise thoughts by letting you know that you are not ready, or you still need to wait upon God's stirring in your heart, or that you will look like a fool if you decide to do this specific thing. Sure, we need God's wisdom and guidance, but if your life is just passing by and you are doing nothing for the kingdom of God, but only being a pew warmer, then you are burying your kingdom assignment, just like the lazy servant did.

Do not lay your responsibility upon the shoulders of God, but make a decision to resist the age-old thief, and to begin to discover your inner kingdom identity. Only as you begin to take some decisive action steps will God then be able to do what He desires to do. Remember, "Faith without works is dead."[2]

Get Your Identity Aligned

If a car is out of alignment, the steering wheel will either turn to the left or to the right. And usually, over time, your tires will wear down faster. Also, if a baseball catcher is not aligned with the pitcher, he will then miss the ball that is thrown to him. You see, one of the devil's main goals is to bring us out of alignment with God which will prevent us from discovering our identity and eventually not fulfilling our purpose on earth.

If you do not know your God-given assignment, then you will be out of spiritual alignment. And you will never successfully or authentically influence others until you discover your inner identity and purpose. This is also true if you want to remain aligned with your identity.

When I was a youth pastor, I discovered a unique individual on social media while I was preparing for a sermon. This person was Nick Vujicic, who is a devout Christian and was born without arms or legs, which is a rare disorder. In one of his speeches he posed a powerful and thought-provoking statement with three particular questions: "Who are you and what your value is? What is your purpose here in life? What is your destiny when you're done?"

Nick continued by saying, "If you don't know the answer of any of those three questions, you're more disabled than I." Wow!

If your spiritual identity is out of alignment, then your faith will be shaky and unstable. This is one of the devil's most powerful goals as he tries to create many road barriers, roadblocks, and numerous demonic potholes for you to be driven through and he attempts to get your life out of alignment with God.

Our goal is to make sure that when these things occur that we always go back to the primary body shop whose master and owner is Christ and He will always give us the best oil change and the best spiritual alignment, so we can continue to stay on the path that He has predestined before us.

Your Identity and Your Purpose Is Not Secure

Having shared so much insight on our God-given identity and purpose, I would not be honest with you if I said that your identity and purpose are secure. No! Your identity and purpose are not secure! In the Scriptures, we have an interesting passage that talks about the talents:

> *For the kingdom of heaven is like a man traveling to a far country, who called his own servants and delivered his goods to them. And to one he gave five talents, to another two, and to another one, to each according to his own ability.*[3]

> *Then he who had received the one talent came and said, "Lord, I knew you to be a hard man, reaping where you have not sown, and gathering where you have not scattered. And I was afraid, and went and hid your talent in the ground. Look, there you have what is yours."*[4]

And now the outcome of this intriguing story:

> *You wicked and lazy servant...So take the talent from him, and give it to him who has ten talents. For to everyone who has, more will be given, and he will have abundance; but from him who does not have, even what he has will be taken away.*[5]

Remember, your destiny has already been chosen and appointed by God, but its fulfillment is decided by you! If this was not the case, then the whole concept of free will would be eradicated. So, as our heavenly Father, God desires for us all to discover and to fulfill our destiny, but many will continue to go to their grave with their identity still lying dormant inside of them.

God has also secured your purpose on this earth and is eagerly waiting for you to step into that purpose, but because of disobedience, lack of discipline, pride, or sin, millions upon millions have aborted their purpose on this earth. And what God has already made secure has become insecure in their personal life.

In the following section, I will outline how you can secure your identity and purpose. But you have to always keep in mind that your future is more important than your past. If you allow your past to grab ahold of you, then it will slowly choke out the God-given future that was already predestined for you.

Your Identity and Purpose Is Only Secure in Christ

Jesus powerfully stated, "I am the vine, you *are* the branches. He who abides in Me, and I in him, bears much fruit; for without Me you can do nothing."[6] Your identity and purpose, and mine, is only secure in Christ. Aside from Him, we cannot bear any kingdom fruit that will be of value or worth. Jesus, continued to expound on this thought by saying, "If you abide in Me, and My words abide in you, you will ask what you desire, and it shall be done for you. By this My Father is glorified, that you bear much fruit; so you will be My disciples."[7]

Just as much as a branch (we are a branch in Christ), cannot bear any fruit by itself, in like manner, we will never be able to fully know, to fully discover, or to fully understand our identity and purpose outside of Christ. This is the number one reason why billions of people around the whole world are in some kind of pursuit, like they are searching for something or for someone. They turn to certain religions, they read specific literature, they go on pilgrimages, they meditate, or they search out numerous religions. In other words, all of humanity feels internally that there is something much more to life than what they see, what they have, and what they know. The one and only answer to all of the above is hidden in Christ, the *True Vine*. And once you discover this truth, only then you will have the guarantee that your identity and purpose is only secure in Christ.

The Truth Versus Your Opinions

Years ago, when so much began to change and shift in our culture and that shift began to infiltrate the church, as a youth pastor, it became a little tough on me to know how I needed to present the truth before the younger generation without being labeled as a religious legalist or a righteous zealot. A lot had to deal with the whole sexual revolution and the legalization of gay marriage, which is now socially labeled as LGBTQ.

What gave me the big breakthrough and the inner freedom on how to distinguish or to discern the difference between the truth and my own opinions or someone else's opinions was to know this fact: I have the full right to share my personal opinions on any subject matter of life including what the Bible has to say, and so does everyone else. This is simply our own free will that God has given to us. But at the end of the day, my opinions or your opinions need to always be referenced and analyzed through the living Scriptures. And if our opinions do not align with the Scriptures, which is the truth, then our opinions are strictly subject to us and to us alone.

The sad and tragic issue here is that many Christians have indoctrinated themselves with their own opinions or have submitted to the opinions of our society, so they will not be labeled as religious bigots or as fanatic Christians who are disconnected from reality and are no longer relevant. And I do agree that in today's fast-paced culture, where the culture is drastically shifting at a rapid pace, that it is not easy for Believers or for the body of Christ. But one of the greatest challenges is not with the new laws or new regulations that are drafted in the disadvantage towards our Judeo-Christian beliefs, but that we have shifted from the fundamental biblical truths and have embraced people's opinions over the truth. And the more we embrace our own opinions or the opinions of the current culture then the less relevant the truth of God will become.

Last time I checked, the Bible was called the book of truth, not the book of opinions! In addition, Jesus spoke plainly and powerfully when He said, "I am the way, the truth, and the life."[8] Let us take a look at some of the most common beliefs or positions that Christians have in today's culture:

- You may have your own opinion of what marriage is or how it needs to be defined, but the Word of God already outlines what marriage is.
- You may have your opinion on abortion or on female rights over their body, but what does the Scripture have to say?
- You may stand by, or support, or have your own opinion on those who live in the LGBTQ lifestyle, but the Bible speaks in plain language about specific lifestyles.
- You may have your own opinion on your sexuality and what you get to do with it, but the holy Scriptures goes into much depth about this subject matter without any reservations.
- You may have your opinions on how you were born or what gender preference you desire, but as the Psalmist said, "I will praise You, for I am fearfully and wonderfully made."[9]

- You may have your opinion on whether hell is real or not, but the Old and the New testament are filled with plenty of references of how real hell is.
- You may have your opinion on sex before marriage, but the book of Proverbs and 1 Corinthians are filled with plenty of Scriptures that relate to sexual purity.
- You may also boldly express your political opinions and beliefs, but the Bible, from cover to cover, demonstrates and illustrates plenty of examples of God's kingdom order and structure and the moral laws that the land needs to live by.

In the court of law, your passionate opinions will hold no weight in comparison to the credible truth, facts, and evidence. In like manner, you could be sincere and genuine in your personal views and beliefs, but that will have no credibility or substance in comparison to the truth. So, the truth of the matter is that many born-again Believers have become passively blinded and even deceived just because they have slowly stepped away from the truth of God's Word and focused more on their personal selfish and self-centered opinions. This is a spiritual symptom which has become very cancerous in our modern-day church culture.

It is this cancerous condition in the body of Christ that has also been causing much confusion, conflicts and contention amongst fellow brothers and sisters in Christ. When your focus veers from the truth, then opinion becomes the next practical option. And for as long as a born-again believer compromises with the truth, then their beliefs and opinions will sound more credible and truthful in their own eyes.

This is dangerous and has also robbed and stripped many Christians from the truth, and now they call it legalism when the Bible calls it *sin*! What the Bible outlines as immoral or perverse, these type of Christians say that times have changed, and God is a God of love. Remember, your opinion is just your opinion and not the truth.

48

WE NEED TO FIGHT FOR THE NEXT GENERATION

W e need to fight for the next generation! This is not meant to be a fancy slogan or an exaggerated statement, but a sobering declaration. The more I observe my kids getting older the more I ponder on their future, and on the future that might be awaiting them. Some days it seems that their future is going to be phenomenal, while other days I am just left speechless.

Yes, every new generation will usher in a move of God like never before! And yes, the generation to come will definitely do much greater things for God's kingdom than any previous generation. I still genuinely believe in that. But, just believing is not enough! The fight for the hearts, the minds, and the souls of our children and the younger generation is real and we as parents, as role models, or as the older generation, need to roll up our sleeves and get into battle-mode.

History Is Repeating Itself Again

In my book *Generating Gap: Raising the Next Generation of Leaders*, I have a chapter which is titled "History Does Repeat Itself." I begin that chapter with Hitler's deadly vision to which most of the world was blindly ignorant until it was too late. Hitler's vison started in captivating the hearts and minds of the youth of his nation. And he succeeded with flawless success.

This same phenomenon is also sweeping though our nation and throughout the world where the academia, the social media, the entertainment industry, and recent political legislations are primarily targeting the innocent hearts and minds of the youth. History is repeating itself again and again and we cannot be ignorant or spiritually blind enough to allow the enemy of our soul to steal the identity of the next generation.

If we remain ignorant and arrogant to history and to the atrocities that occurred throughout history, then we will set ourselves up for much grief and much heart ache. Just as Hitler craftily captivated the hearts and minds of the youth in his nation, today, we likewise have many pied pipers that are luring our sons and daughters towards the path of destruction. And if we are not alert and ignore the discernment of the Holy Spirit, then we are destined to repeat history again and again.

Un-Brainwash the Brainwashed

Society has a name for you! Your friends and co-workers have a name for you! And your family members and relatives have a name for you! The question is, do you know who you are?

I would be labeled as a liar and an uninformed individual if I told you that our modern-day progressive society is not brainwashing our children and the younger generation. The truth is that too much brainwashing has already occurred and as parents, as church leaders, and as the children of God, we need to roll up our sleeves and begin to apply the truth of God's Word as living water to the hearts and minds of the younger generation.

If you carefully follow the social media trends, the cable news, and some of the most talked about issues amongst the younger generation, then you will be very surprised about the issues that most concern them, and based on these issues they are standing in support for a particular 2020 presidential candidate, as I write this. They are concerned for climate change, free education, having their college tuition fully paid off by the government, freedom over their bodies to do whatever they want, more rights for diversity and marriage equality, and the advancement of socialism. These were just a few key components to their ideology, which is fed to them by those who are trying to strip away our democracy and freedom, and they do these things by brainwashing the younger generation to focus more on the importance of saving the earth, instead of saving an unborn child. They focus more on free handouts instead of teaching the younger generation to roll up their sleeves and work hard to achieve greatness and success. And these same elites both from within the government and those who possess much money are polluting the innocent hearts of the younger generation and shifting their focus more on temporary pleasures instead of on long term commitments.

As parents, as church leaders, and as role models we need to un-brainwash the brainwashed and help them to see the greater purpose that God has already designed before them. And we need to teach our children and the younger generation that God has designed and orchestrated everything in a divine and perfect way, but if we resist or go against the original design or ordinances of God, then we place ourselves directly into opposition of our

Maker and our Creator, which makes us a child of disobedience and this will have treacherous consequences.

Parents, Please Wake Up and Smell the Coffee of Reality

I by no means declare myself as a perfect parent or the leading voice of the one who is most concerned for the younger generation, but my heart and spirit man is continually stirred with much passion to see the next generation of kingdom leaders rise up and make a kingdom impact in this world. With that said, I do want to yell from the bosom of my heart for parents to please wake up and to smell the coffee of reality!

Parents play the most critical role in the fight for the next generation. Parents are the most qualified coaches, mentors, role models, and teachers. Parents obtain the kingdom command and the right to raise and to prepare their son or daughter for their kingdom assignment on this earth. And no one else can truly fulfill the role of the parent in the life of their child. There are some exceptions to this, but God knew exactly what He was doing when He created the original family unit.

Are You a Role Model or a Stumbling Block?

Our children and the younger generation are already being bombarded on a daily basis through all the nonsense that takes place through social media and through the academia. The last thing they need is for adults or their parents to become a stumbling block to their spiritual growth and development.

I often talk to my two eldest children in regard to the importance of what kind of family culture we have and what kind of family values we live by since there is so much poison in the atmosphere in many families that are actually hurting the child. It may be excusable for those parents who do not know the Lord or who do not possess a personal relationship with Jesus to create a toxic environment for their child, but there is absolutely no excuse for those parents who consider themselves to be born-again Christians and have a toxic environment in their family. It is also inexcusable for these Christian parents to become a stumbling block instead of a role model to their child.

Because of my parent's background and the cultural limitations that they had when we immigrated to America it is justifiable up to a certain degree on how they were limited in investing into their seven children. But they did their best to sow the Word of God into our lives and be those needed Godly role models. But they also practiced a good amount of religious legalism that became like a stumbling block to my faith and to my understanding of God's greater purpose for my life. As a parent of three, I desperately need God's wisdom and counsel in raising, disciplining, equipping, and setting my children on the path and the purpose that God has predestined for them. Sure, it is not an easy task, but our position as parents needs to be as role models to our children and not as stumbling blocks.

You Were Born for Greatness

"You were born for greatness" may sound like a cliché, but from God's perspective, it is not! We are living in a world where on one hand you hear some say that we were born for greatness, while on the other hand our society is grooming individuals with a herd mentality. Take a look at the illustration below to further understand my point:

Born in the town of Plainville.
Grew up in the town of Plainville.
Graduated in the town of Plainville.
Got married in the town of Plainville.
Bought my first home in the town of Plainville.
Raised my family in the town of Plainville.
Never left the town of Plainville.
Died and got buried in the town of Plainville.

The above illustration portrays the life of many and then we wonder why so many of us are very bored, miserable, and spiritually stagnant. Remember, you were born for greatness! So, live a life of purpose! Get out of your comfort zone! Turn your life into an adventure! And when you personally have discovered that you were born and created for greatness, only then you will be able to impact, to direct, to influence, and to become the needed role model, a spiritual mentor, and a fighter for your children and for the next generation.

49
FACTS VERSUS THE TRUTH

In our journey of life, we will be continually confronted with facts but those facts are not necessarily the truth. Let us take a look at the most common facts that will continually attack, challenge, and even oppose your God-given identity and purpose. But no matter how loudly these facts scream into your spiritual ears, these facts are not necessarily the truth.

Facts Versus the Truth

Let us take a look at some of the most common facts that people often turn into their truths, which end up detouring them from their kingdom purpose and assignment on this earth:

- *Fact:* You are young and inexperienced.
  The Truth: Lying dormant within your heart and spirit is potential that needs to be released.
- *Fact:* Right now, you do not have the finances to fulfill your God-given purpose and assignment.
  The Truth: If God appointed you and equipped you for this specific assignment, He will also become your Jehovah Jireh.
- *Fact:* Many are bullied for how they look, or for who they are, which could result in the individual hurting or even killing themselves.
  The Truth: You are fearfully and wonderfully made.
- *Fact:* Many struggle with their sexuality and gender identity.
  The Truth: The Word of God declares, "For You formed my inward parts; You covered me in my mother's womb."[1]
- *Fact:* Your current job sucks and you are miserable there.
  The Truth: Your job is just a preparation for your purpose.
- *Fact:* You may not have the needed finances to accomplish or fulfill your kingdom assignment.
  The Truth: Since God has called and ordained you, He will also provide everything that you will need to accomplish your purpose on this earth.

One of the greatest challenges to why born-again Believers struggle to discern what is *fact* and what is *truth* is because there are not allowing the Holy Spirit that abides in them to become their personal Helper. Jesus made a profound statement in regards to the Holy Spirit, "And I will pray the Father, and He will give you another Helper, that He may abide with you forever—the Spirit of truth, whom the world cannot receive, because it neither sees Him nor knows Him; but you know Him, for He dwells with you and will be in you."[2]

It is very important that we grasp the powerful truth that the Holy Spirit is our Helper and He is also called the *Spirit of truth.*[3] You see, every day we are continually barraged with facts, which overtime become our truths and as a result, we become discouraged, distracted, dismayed, and eventually detoured from our kingdom path. The point here is not for you to dismiss or to become naïve to these facts of life, but for you to turn to the Spirit of Truth, who is your Helper, and He will speak to you the truth, He will show you what is true, He will guide you to the path of truth, and He will transform your life through the truth of God's living Word.

Made in the Image and Likeness of God

Many are aware that a major part of the products purchased in the US are produced in China, but the product that is made in the USA is typically more expensive and has higher quality. The truth is, none of us were made in the USA, or Europe, or Asia, or China, or Canada! You might have been born in one of those countries but if we were to check your spiritual brand imprint, then it would say, "Made in The Image and Likeness of God!"

Fish were designed to swim! Birds were designed to fly! Cars were designed to drive! Pens were designed to write! And lightbulbs were designed to shine light! But the big question is, what were you designed to do on this earth? You see, to be made in the image and in the likeness of God means that you and I possess the characteristics, the attributes, the nature, and the traits of God.

Every manufacturer or designer has a specific purpose and a specific function for which their product was designed. Our heavenly Father, our Creator, has also placed within each and every living human being a specific purpose that each individual needs to fulfill while we are still alive on this earth.

As we go through life, we are pummeled on a daily basis with specific information, with factual analysis, with people's opinions, and other nonsense, which results in the truth becoming more diluted in our hearts, in our minds, and in our lives. In other words, what the Creator has originally created us to do, now begins to malfunction in our lives and this eventually results in a spiritual identity crisis.

Again, remember these truthful principles: eagles do not fly with chickens! Lions do not hunt with house cats! Horses do not jump with donkeys! Dolphins do not swim with sharks! And cheetahs do not run with turtles! And you will never see an eagle building its nest in a chicken coop or see a chicken flying as high as an eagle. Why? Because each one was specifically designed by the Creator for a specific purpose and with unique characteristics that separate each animal from one another. And in like manner, your Creator has created you with unique abilities, skills, talents, and potential that differentiate you from your fellow peers and make you a valuable asset to this world and to the kingdom of God.

God Is Not in the Business of Making Average People

Do you eat an average meal at a restaurant? Do you enjoy watching an average movie? Do you want to have average friends? Do you want to have an average career? And would you want to have an average marriage? Most likely no! In like manner, God is not in the business of making average people, with average gifts, and with average potential.

Since we are continually surrounded with average people who have average thinking, we tend to blend in with these same crowds like a chameleon. But God's original intention was for us to stand out from this average crowd like a zebra posing the question, "Am I black with white stripes or white with black stripes?"

You see, your originality and uniqueness of who you are automatically makes you a valuable asset to the world, to your family, to your marriage, to your local church, to your occupation, and to your society. So, do not delay in allowing everyone to discover who you are and what untapped potential lies within you.

What God Sees Versus What People See

One of the tragic issues in the body of Christ is that we often allow people to define who we are instead of allowing our Creator to define who we are. For example:

- David's brothers saw a sheep herder, but God saw a giant slayer and a king of Israel.
- Joseph's brothers saw a childish dreamer, but God saw a powerful influencer who would become second in command and save millions from starvation.
- Christian Jews saw killer Saul, but God saw Apostle Paul who would also write most of the New Testament.
- Jesus' neighbors saw an ordinary carpenter, but God saw the Savior of the world.
- Joseph saw his bride, Mary, pregnant with a child and wanted to break off their marriage out of fear and humiliation, but God saw the mother to His Son, Jesus, who would reconcile all of humanity back to its Creator.

The question is, who are you allowing to define your purpose, your destiny, and your calling? The issue again is if an individual is wearing yellow colored glasses, then they see everything in yellow color. Or if they are wearing green colored glasses, then in like manner, everything to their naked eye is green. So, what happens when you allow a selfish, self-centered, or narrow minded individual to explain what they see in you? Whatever beliefs, convictions, or limited theological thinking they possess will become their evaluation or analysis of who they think you are.

If we are able to lay aside the perception others have of us and allow our Creator to define or to explain who we are, then everything will become crystal clear. Why? Because our heavenly Father does not wear any humanistic or manmade glasses. And what He sees is not what people see in us.

Your Excuses Will Never Exonerate You

Throughout the Bible we read passages of Jeremiah, Moses, Gideon, and others alike who would try to offer God a bunch of lame excuses on why they were not qualified for their God-given assignment. In like manner, many Christians Believers do the exact same thing and one of their main excuses is that they think they are not fit or qualified for their purpose and calling. Let us take a look at some biblical characters who were the least qualified candidates:

- *Moses* was a murderer and a stutterer.
- *Peter* denied Christ three times and also had a big mouth.
- *Saul (Apostle Paul)* was a religious zealot who murdered and persecuted Christians.

- *Jonah* ran away from his assignment.
- *King David* took another man's wife, got her pregnant, and eventually killed her husband.
- *Apostle Thomas* doubted Jesus' resurrection.
- *Jacob* made a profession out of lying.
- *Elijah* dropped his ministry because of fear and went into hiding in a cave.
- *Rahab* the harlot was a professional prostitute.
- *Samson* was a womanizer.
- *Noah* got drunk and laid naked in his tent.
- *Abraham* and *Sarah* were too old and beyond their prime years.
- *Gideon* was full of fear and doubt.
- *Jeremiah* complained that he was too young.
- The *Samaritan woman* had five husbands and was currently living with her boyfriend.
- The *disciples* fell asleep in the Garden of Gethsemane while Jesus had asked them to stand in agreement of prayer with Him as He went through His most difficult spiritual warfare with Satan.

So, what is your excuse for not allowing God to use you for His kingdom purpose? What is stopping you from discovering your identity *in* Christ and your identity *through* Christ? You see, your mind is like a womb and your thoughts are like a sperm. How you see yourself, what you think about yourself, and the belief that you have about yourself will determine what you give birth to in your life. *Can I See Your ID?,* is not meant to stir your curiosity, but to stir your inner spirit man so that you will become passionate for who you are and for what purpose you were born on this earth. And Apostle Paul encourages us with these words, "Therefore do not be ashamed of the testimony of our Lord, nor of me His prisoner, but share with me in the suffering for the gospel according to the power of God, who has saved us and called *us* with a holy calling, not according to our works, but according to His own purpose and grace which was given to us in Christ Jesus before time began."[4] So, know your kingdom identity and purpose and become that original masterpiece that your heavenly Father has created you to be.

50
God Is the Author of Your Life

One of the most astounding truths is that our heavenly Father, His Son Jesus, and the Holy Spirit are the *authors* and the *finishers* of our life.[1] And His promises to us as it is written in Isaiah are concrete and assuring when He said, "For My thoughts *are* not your thoughts, nor *are* your ways My ways," says the Lord. "For *as* the heavens are higher than the earth, so are My ways higher than your ways, and My thoughts than your thoughts."[2] And God is faithful to His word and to all of His promises, as He again reassured us with these powerful word, "So shall My word be that goes forth from My mouth; it shall not return to Me void, but it shall accomplish what I please, and it shall prosper *in the thing* for which I sent it."[3] Wow! Now that is a guarantee that we all can take and cash in at the bank of life!

God is the author of your life and He will stand behind His own Word. He will do all that He needs to do in order to ensure that His Word that has already been released into your life comes to pass. This is a profound truth that we as God's children need to grasp in our hearts, our minds, and in our spirit man. So, once again I pose this vital question:

Can I See Your ID?

Yes, You Can See My ID!

Notes

All scriptural references come from New King James Version (NKJV), unless otherwise noted.

Chapter 1: Can I See Your ID?
1. www.dictionary.com (identification)
2. Genesis 1:26-27

Chapter 2: It All Began in the Garden
1. Genesis 3:1b
2. Genesis 3:11
3. Genesis 3:1
4. Genesis 3:1b

Chapter 4: The Identity of Adam and Eve
1. Genesis 2:19a
2. Genesis 2:19b

Chapter 5: The Identity of Cain
1. Genesis 4:7a
2. Gal. 2:16

Chapter 7: The Identity of Abraham and Sarah
1. Genesis 22:1-2
2. 1 Samuel 17:39
3. Job 1:14-19

Chapter 8: The Identity of Lot
1. Genesis 13:10
2. Genesis 19:2
3. Gen 19:7-8

Chapter 9: The Identity of Esau
1. Genesis 27:41
2. Matthew 16:26
3. Ecclesiastes 3:1-8

Chapter 10: The Identity of Jacob
1. Genesis 32:28a
2. Genesis 32:26a
3. Genesis 32:26b

Chapter 11: The Identity of Joseph
1. Proverbs 16:18
2. Proverbs 18:16
3. Genesis 50:19-20

Chapter 12: The Identity of Amram and Jochebed
1. Exodus 2:3-6 AMP
2. Exodus 1:22
3. Exodus 2:2 NLT

Chapter 13: The Identity of Moses
1. Exodus 3:6
2. 2 Timothy 1:7
3. Proverbs 16:9
4. Deuteronomy 34:9

Chapter 14: The Identity of Joshua and Caleb
1. Joshua 14:11

2. Joshua 24:15

Chapter 15: The Identity of Rahab
1. https://www.thesaurus.com/browse/prostitute?s=t

Chapter 16: The Identity of Gideon
1. Judges 6:11-27
2. Matthew 16:19b
3. Deuteronomy 28:13a
4. 1 Peter 2:9
5. Judges 6:11-17 (excerpts)

Chapter 17: The Identity of Samson
1. 1 Corinthians 12:4-7
2. 1 Samuel 16:7
3. Judges 16:15

Chapter 18: The Identity of Naomi and Ruth
1. Ruth 1:13b
2. Ruth 1:13)

Chapter 21: The Identity of King Saul
1. 1 Samuel 15:24b
2. 1 Samuel 15:30
3. 1 Samuel 31:4b
4. Robin Williams, National Center for Biotechnology Information 2016, July-Sept (https://www.ncbi.nlm.nih.gov/pubmed/27737312)
5. 1 Samuel 16:14-16
6. Jeremiah 29:11 (AMP)

Chapter 22: The Identity of David
1. 1 Samuel 16:11
2. 1 Samuel 16:7b

Chapter 23: The Identity of Shammah, Eleazar, Josheb-Basshebeth, Abishai, and Benaiah
1. 1 Corinthians 12:1-11
2. 1 Corinthians 12:4-7

Chapter 24: The Identity of Absalom
1. Proverbs 17:22
2. Matthew 18:22
3. Exodus 20:12

Chapter 25: The Identity of Solomon
1. Proverbs 1:7
2. Proverbs 9:10
3. Proverbs 14:26
4. Proverbs 14:27
5. Proverbs 15:33
6. Proverbs 16: 6b
7. Proverbs 19:23a

8. 1 Corinthians 8:1
Chapter 26: The Identity of Elijah
1. 1 Peter 5:8
Chapter 27: The Identity of Jezebel
2. Revelation 2:20 & 2:23
3. 1 John 2:16
4. 2 Timothy 3:1-5
Chapter 28: The Identity of Elisha
1. 2 Kings 2:9
Chapter 29: The Identity of a Young Jewish Girl
1. 2 King 5:5
Chapter 31: The Identity of Nehemiah
1. Nehemiah 6:15
Chapter 32: The Identity of Mordecai
1. Esther 2:23
2. Esther 6:3
3. Esther 6:3a
4. Esther 6:11b
5. Malachi 3:16
6. Esther 7:9-10 & 9:14
Chapter 33: The Identity of Esther
1. Esther 4:14b
2. Esther 2:15b
Chapter 34: The Identity of Job
1. Job 1:9
Chapter 35: The Identity of Daniel
1. Romans 11:29
2. Revelation 3:16
3. Matthew 17:21
Chapter 36: The Identity of Shadrach, Meshach, and Abed-Nego
1. Daniel 1
2. Daniel 1:5
Chapter 37: The Identity of Jonah
1. Jeremiah 29:11
2. Jonah 1:6
Chapter 38: The Identity of John the Baptist
1. Luke 7:28)
2. Matthew 3:3b
3. Mark 1:7
4. Matthew 11:3
Chapter 39: The Identity of Virgin Mary
1. Luke 1:27b
2. 1 Thessalonians 4:3-5 (NIV)
3. 1 Corinthians 6:18
Chapter 40: The Identity of Apostle Thomas
1. John 20:25
Chapter 42: The Identity of the Prodigal Son
1. https://www.dictionary.com/brows e/prodigal?s=t

Chapter 43: The Identity of Apostle Paul
1. Acts 9:4a
2. Acts 9:5a
3. Acts 9:5b
4. Acts 9:5c
5. Acts 9:6
6. 1 Corinthians 11:24
7. 1 Corinthians 11:25
8. Acts 14:19
9. 1 Corinthians 11:25
10. 1 Corinthians 11:26
11. 1 Corinthians 11:27
12. Ephesians 4:1-3
Chapter 45: The Identity of Lucifer
1. Isaiah 14:13-14
2. Matthew 12:25
3. John 10:10a
4. John 8:44
5. 1 John 4:4
Chapter 46: The Identity of Jesus
1. Genesis 1:26
2. Matthew 4:3
3. Matthew 4:6
4. Matthew 4:9
5. Matt 13:54-55
6. Luke 4:24
7. Mark 6:4
8. Hebrews 13:8
9. John 15:5
10. Romans 6:3-5
11. Matthew 12:46-47
12. John 7:3-5
13. Matthew 16:13b (NLT)
Chapter 47: The Age-Old Thief
1. John 10:10a
2. James 2:20
3. Matthew 25:14-15
4. Matthew 25:24-25
5. Matthew 25:26a, 28-29
6. John 15:5
7. John 15: 7-8
8. John 14:6
9. Psalm 139:14
Chapter 49: Facts Versus the Truth
1. Psalm 139:13
2. John 14:16-17
3. John 15:26
4. 2 Timothy 1:8-9
Chapter 50: God Is the Author of Your Life
5. Hebrews 12:2
6. Isaiah 55:8-9
7. Isaiah 55:11

ABOUT THE AUTHOR

Stan Belyshev is an entrepreneur, author, life coach, and a vlogger. Stan and his wife Lyudmila and three children, Justin, Angelina, and Juliana reside in Greater Atlanta and are members at Free Chapel. Having served as a youth pastor for ten years in the state of Massachusetts, Stan is passionate about discipling and equipping the next generation of kingdom leaders through his book publications, podcasts, YouTube channel, and one-on-one coaching and mentoring.

"How many people will be better off because of who you are and what value and worth you could add to their life."

Other Books by the Author

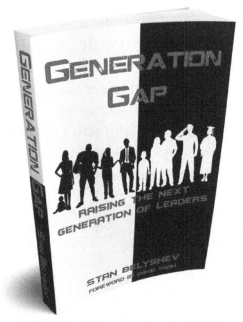

Relevant and Practical Ways on how to Disciple, Coach, Mentor, and Connect with the Next Generation (Ages 15 to 30)!

- Discover the nine most influential role models and mind molders that are currently discipling and shaping the hearts and minds of the younger generation!
- Rediscover the true purpose of discipleship the way Jesus portrayed it to His twelve disciples, which is coaching and mentoring in a personal way!
- Relevant and practical ways to reach out and to engage the younger generation in your church!
- Radical and Biblical insight on captivating the hearts of the 15 to 30 year-old (Gen-Y and Gen-Z) in your church and in your community!
- Uncover and grasp one of the main missing links between the older generation and the younger generation, which is the absentee of Spiritual Fathers and Mothers in the body of Christ!
- As a parent, as a pastor, as a church leader or as a young adult, become that genuine role model to the next generation which is rising up!
- Why the older generation continually struggles to connect and to understand the younger generation!
- Discover the crafty tactics of the devil, which are masqueraded in technology, education, movies, books and social networks that are molding the hearts and minds of our children and the younger generation!

Made in the USA
Columbia, SC
10 February 2021